How to Read Theology for All Its Worth provides an excellent guide to the often confusing landscape of theology. Karin Stetina writes with energy and clarity, drawing on her extensive knowledge of major theologians and philosophers. Her quick-paced prose, coupled with effective illustrations, will benefit both the pastor and student who desire to know God and themselves better.

Lynn H. Cohick, provost/dean, Denver Seminary

Professor Stetina is a highly respected colleague of mine. She is known as being well-read in her field of historical theology and church history, and she is an excellent communicator. So it comes as no surprise that this marvelous book is a combination of high-quality and relevant content with an easy-to-read, practical style. I love the fact that Stetina views theology as it should be viewed—as a branch of *knowledge*. Consequently, she takes it very seriously. And the selection of topics is foundational to further study. In fact, I know of no other book that focuses on the specific range of prolegomena to theology like this one does. I wish I would have had this book available before I went to seminary. Laypeople and students alike will learn how to be discerning readers in theology if they read *How to Read Theology for All Its Worth*. I highly recommend it.

J. P. Moreland, distinguished professor of philosophy, Talbot School of Theology, Biola University, and author of *Love Your God With All Your Mind*

This book may well be the first of its kind—at least I know of no other like it. My friend and former colleague Karin Stetina has produced a remarkably insightful and practical guide for students of theology. Reading theology today can be a daunting task, with no clear road signs to direct us or warnings about whom and what to avoid. This book is precisely what the Christian world has needed—a wise, fair-minded, objective handbook on what questions to ask when reading theology. I have a strong sense that this extremely helpful work will be the standard reference guide for years to come.

Sam Storms, Bridgeway Church,
Oklahoma City, Oklahoma

Karin Stetina's latest work equips readers of theology with useful and effective approaches for becoming discerning readers without leaving faith convictions at the door. This insightful and accessible book will surely become a staple for theology students who value sound method in the development of their work.

Jennifer Powell McNutt, Franklin S. Dyrness
associate professor in biblical and theological
studies, Wheaton College

How to Read
Theology
for All Its Worth

How to Read
Theology
for All Its Worth

A Guide for Students

Karin Spiecker Stetina

ZONDERVAN
ACADEMIC

ZONDERVAN ACADEMIC

How to Read Theology for All Its Worth
Copyright © 2020 by Karin Spiecker Stetina

Requests for information should be addressed to:
Zondervan, *3900 Sparks Dr. SE, Grand Rapids, Michigan 49546*

ISBN 978-0-310-09382-4 (softcover)

ISBN 978-0-310-09383-1 (ebook)

Cover photography: © *EmirMemedovski / Getty Images*
Interior design: Kait Lamphere

Printed in the United States of America

20 21 22 23 24 25 26 27 28 /LSC/ 13 12 11 10 9 8 7 6 5 4 3 2 1

I dedicate this book and all of my work
to my Lord and Savior, Jesus Christ,
who is the reason I am a theologian.

Therefore, as you received Christ Jesus the Lord, so walk in him, rooted and built up in him and established in the faith, just as you were taught, abounding in thanksgiving.

COLOSSIANS 2:6–7

Contents

Acknowledgments xi
Preface xiii

Introduction: Becoming a Student of Theology 1

1. Overview: Getting Acquainted with the Tools of
   the Discerning Reader 9
2. Preparing for Reading Theology for All Its Worth:
   Being Steeped in Prayer and Scripture 21
3. First Steps: Examining Textual Features and
   Publication Information 31
4. Identifying the Context: Getting Better Acquainted
   with the Theologian 51
5. Discerning Theological Frameworks: Identifying
   the Theme of the Work and How It Is Conveyed 71
6. Discovering the Sources: Identifying the
   Foundations of the Work 89
7. Discerning the Theologian's View: Listening for
   the Main Contention, Key Points, and Key Terms . . 109
8. Assessing: Evaluating and Applying the
   Theological Work 125

Appendix 1: Equipping Others to Read Theology for All
   Its Worth 147

Appendix 2: A Selected List of Significant Theologians
and Theological Works. 159
Appendix 3: How to Dialogue with a Theological Work . . . 171
Appendix 4: A Guide for Participating in a Theological
Discussion. 173
Appendix 5: How to Lead a Theological Discussion 177
Appendix 6: Theological Discussion Questions on
Cyprian's On the Unity of the Church 183
Glossary 185
General Index. 199

Acknowledgments

I am grateful to all the people who have contributed to this work, particularly Joanne Jung and my fellow colleagues at Talbot School of Theology—Erik Thoennes, Leon Harris, Andy Draycott, Rob Lister, Thaddeus Williams, and John McKinley—who encouraged me to pursue this project. Also to Uche Anizor, Doug Huffman, and Doug Geivett, who made important contributions to the development of various chapters.

A special thanks to my brother Eric Spiecker and my brilliant friend Kristy Wellman Reardon for helping me proof an early draft. Also to my dear friends Mary Vosburg, Ginny Barta, Manya Gyuro, Darcy Faitel, and Paula Wilding for being my cheering section in life. Without you, I would have never had the courage to take on this project.

I am grateful to Biola University and Talbot School of Theology for giving me a research leave in the fall of 2018 to complete the manuscript. I also appreciate Langham Literature, a publishing ministry of Langham Partnership, for allowing me to utilize and expand on my chapter titled "Equipping Students to Read Theology with Discernment," in *Thinking Theologically about Language Teaching*, edited by Cheri Pierson and Will Bankston.

Madison Trammel and the Zondervan team, thanks for your excitement from the very beginning about this project and your valuable assistance along the way.

Finally, to my family—you have been patient and loving as I spent long hours laboring over this project.

Theology is a serious quest for the true knowledge of God, undertaken in response to his self-revelation, illumined by Christian tradition, manifesting a rational inner coherence, issuing in ethical conduct, resonating with the contemporary world and concerned for the greater glory of God.

JOHN STOTT, "THEOLOGY:
A MULTIDIMENSIONAL DISCIPLINE"

An intelligent heart acquires knowledge,
and the ear of the wise seeks knowledge.

PROVERBS 18:15

Preface

In the church of Jesus Christ there can and should be no non-theologians.

KARL BARTH, *KARL BARTH LETTERS, 1961–68*

Whether we acknowledge it or not, we are all theologians. We all have convictions about God and creation, and we read Scripture according to these convictions. The real question isn't *if* we are theologians, but rather if we are *good* theologians. Are we faithfully discovering and proclaiming true knowledge that emerges out of accurately hearing, interpreting, and living out God's Word?

Prior to college, I had never heard the word *theology* and was completely unaware that faithful, Bible-believing Christians held different perspectives on Scripture. My theological approach was very simple: read the Bible and try to do what it says, sometimes with prayer added to the mix. As a college freshman, I took a course titled "Christian Doctrine" and began to realize that faithful followers of Christ did not always interpret passages in the same way.

As I stayed up late at night discussing with my classmates whether God predestines us to heaven or whether we freely choose Christ, I became aware that my simplistic approach could not stand up to such a challenging question. My professor assigned us readings from Saint Augustine to help us through the labyrinth of what he called "the predestination versus free will debate." Unfortunately, Augustine left me even more confused than I had been before. I may as well have been reading Greek. I don't think I am alone in this experience. Although my high school Great Books seminar had taught me how to read the classics, I had put those tools of reading aside when reading the Bible or theology, believing that faith should be simple and straightforward.

It wasn't until I sat down to write my master's thesis that I truly began to feel equipped to be guided by Christian tradition, thereby allowing the "great cloud of witnesses" (Hebrews 12:1 NIV) to aid me in interpreting Scripture. I now realize, however, that one need not wait to write a master's thesis in order to learn to read theology with wisdom and discernment. This book seeks to train students in the art of reading theology with the hope that they may be able to understand and appreciate it for all its worth.

Many people have contributed to my training in reading theology, including my high school Great Books teacher, Mrs. Schwalbach. She introduced me to Mortimer Adler's *How to Read a Book* and gave me a love for the classics and Socratic discussions. I am also grateful for Dorothy Sayers's *The Lost Tools of Learning*, C. S. Lewis's *The Abolition of Man*, and Charlotte Mason's pioneering works on education. These works have helped me recognize the importance of training my head, heart, and hands to think about, love, and do what is good, pure, and true and to see books as great partners in my Christian journey. My professors in undergraduate and graduate school—Frank A. James III, Mark Noll, Alister McGrath, Timothy Phillips, Dennis Okholm, Kenneth Hagen, and Patrick Carey—were also formative in teaching me how to be illumined by Scripture and to value the Christian tradition.

The greatest teacher of all, however, is the Holy Spirit, who is the arbiter of truth (1 Corinthians 2:6–16; 1 John 2:20, 27) and the seal of our redemption by Christ (Ephesians 1:13–14). It is my hope that this short practical guide will help the reader in what John Stott calls the "serious quest for the true knowledge of God." If you are convinced of *why* you should read theology, my hope is that this work will help you with the *how*.[1]

---

1. This work was developed out of a chapter titled "Equipping Students to Read Theology with Discernment," in *Thinking Theologically about Language Teaching: Christian Perspectives on an Educational Calling*, ed. Cheri L. Pierson and Will Bankston (Carlisle, UK: Langham Global Library, 2017). It has been greatly expanded and published with permission of Karin Spiecker Stetina and Langham Literature, a publishing ministry of Langham Partnership.

Becoming a Student of Theology

When you listen and read one thinker, you become a clone . . . Two thinkers, you become confused . . . Ten thinkers, you'll begin developing your own voice . . . Two or three hundred thinkers, you become wise.

TIM KELLER, "BECOMING WISE"

Whoever walks with the wise becomes wise,
but the companion of fools will suffer harm.

PROVERBS 13:20

THE TASK OF A THEOLOGY STUDENT

Many people are intimidated or bored by theology, seeing it as a subject for the academy or as an "ivory tower" discipline that has little to do with daily life. However, we are all theologians, whether we recognize it or not. We all have beliefs about the nature of God, humanity's relation to God, and religious truth. The question is whether or not we are good theologians. As Christians, we are all called to be good theologians—to adhere to and proclaim biblically based teachings, or what Scripture calls "sound doctrine." We are to be prepared at all times to proclaim the truth about the way things really are and live out that truth as students of God's Word (2 Timothy 4:1–5).

A student of theology, as Helmut Thielicke points out in his classic text *A Little Exercise for Young Theologians,* is called not only to intellectually understand Christian doctrine but also to pursue an active faith that fosters love. He warns the young theologian that "theology is a very human business, a craft, and sometimes an art. In the last analysis it is always ambivalent. It can be sacred theology or diabolical theology. That depends on the hands and hearts which further it."[1] One of the most pressing questions is "How does one discern the truth communicated in the theology we read?" Learning how to answer this question is one of the primary tasks of the student of theology.

True learning, in general, requires that one go beyond merely understanding the words printed on the page in the pursuit of knowledge. Christian learning is unique in that its ultimate purpose is not just knowledge, but godly wisdom. In *The Discipline of Spiritual Discernment,* Tim Challies

---

1. Helmut Thielicke, *A Little Exercise for Young Theologians* (Grand Rapids: Eerdmans, 1988), 37.

acknowledges this, writing that the goal is "to better know, understand, and serve God."[2]

Furthermore, when we truly know who God is, we have the opportunity to know who we are. John Calvin emphasizes this idea in the opening of his *Institutes of the Christian Religion*, which he wrote to instruct students of theology in the study of Scripture, by testifying to the fact that genuine wisdom comprises true knowledge of God and of self.[3] Knowledge of God and knowledge of self are inextricably linked. We can only have an accurate understanding of self if we know our Creator and Redeemer. The reverse is true as well. Calvin also warns that we are not to be satisfied with mere speculative knowledge:

> We ought to observe that we are called to a knowledge of God: not that knowledge which, content with empty speculation, merely flits in the brain, but that which will be sound and fruitful if we duly perceive it, and if it takes root in the heart . . . The most perfect way of seeking God, and the most suitable order, is not for us to attempt with bold curiosity to penetrate to the investigation of his essence, which we ought more to adore than meticulously to search out, but for us to contemplate him in his works whereby he renders himself near and familiar to us, and in some manner communicates himself.[4]

Real knowledge of God, for Calvin, comes through contemplating God in his works.

As Calvin correctly suggests, godly wisdom is not empty speculation, nor is it merely gaining knowledge from a teacher

---

2. Tim Challies, *The Discipline of Spiritual Discernment* (Wheaton, IL: Crossway, 2007), 55.

3. John Calvin, *Institutes of the Christian Religion*, Library of Christian Classics, vol. XX and XXI, ed. John T. McNeill (Philadelphia: Westminster, 1960), I.1.1 (hereafter, *Inst.*).

4. *Inst.*, I.5.9.

to become an expert in your own right. Instead, it involves a twofold knowledge of God and ourselves that takes root in the heart and is lived out in faith. Furthermore, as Scripture teaches, *wisdom*, unlike worldly knowledge, recognizes our need to rely on Christ through the power of the Holy Spirit.

Paul suggests this, praying for the Ephesians "that Christ may dwell in" their hearts "through faith—that you, being rooted and grounded in love, may have strength to comprehend with all the saints what is the breadth and length and height and depth, and to know the love of Christ that surpasses knowledge, that you may be filled with all the fullness of God" (Ephesians 3:17–19). How can a Christian practically pursue this godly wisdom? In particular, how can one learn to recognize, understand, and respond to God's truth?

THE WORD AS OUR SOURCE OF TRUTH

The short answer is God's Word. As Christians, we are called to live a life informed by God's Word. Psalm 119 (NIV) declares the beauty and value of God's Word, opening with the words "Blessed are those whose ways are blameless, who walk according to the law of the LORD." The psalmist cries out, "Teach me, LORD, the way of your decrees, that I may follow it to the end. Give me understanding, so that I may keep your law and obey it with all my heart" (verses 33–34). He continues, "Your word is a lamp for my feet, a light on my path" (verse 105). The author later cries out, "[God,] give me discernment that I may understand your statutes" (verse 125). The psalmist recognizes the vital importance of God's Word and turns to it for understanding and direction (verses 130–133). While the source of light and wisdom is apparent, the understanding and application of it are not always as obvious.

How do we accurately interpret God's Word? Often we turn to theologians, pastors, friends, and even the internet as our guides. In a world inundated with resources that are just a few keystrokes away, one of the challenges we face is deciding *to whom* we should listen. Pastor and theologian Tim Keller rightly recognizes the importance of this question:

> When you listen and read one thinker, you become a clone. If you really spend a lot of time listening and reading two thinkers, you become confused. If you really spend a lot of time in reading and listening to about ten thinkers, you'll start to develop your own voice. And if you listen and read two or three hundred thinkers, you become wise and develop your voice.[5]

What if, for example, we want to understand the biblical concept of justification? Should we listen to Martin Luther, or to the teachings from the Roman Catholic Church at the Council of Trent? Are we justified by faith alone, or by faith *and* works? Before we can begin to answer the question *to whom* we should listen, or who will help us "become wise and develop your voice," we need to examine *how* we are to listen. Being a good listener, or what I will call here a discerning reader, is vital to being able to determine that. Unfortunately, this skill has become virtually a lost art.

BIBLICAL CALL TO DISCERNMENT

In his letter to the Philippians, Paul implores the church to think about whatever is true, honorable, just, pure, commendable, excellent, and praiseworthy (Philippians 4:8). He is calling Christians to godly thinking. As Proverbs 23:7 (KJV)

---

5. Tim Keller, "Doing Justice," lecture at Reform and Resurge Conference (May 2006); for a shorter version, see Tim Keller, "Daily Keller: Wisdom from Tim Keller 365 Days a Year," May 17, 2017, http://dailykeller.com/category /wisdom.

points out, *what* a person thinks, a person *is*. Scripture teaches that the things we choose to dwell on will impact who we are. The early American theologian Jonathan Edwards makes a similar point in his book *Freedom of the Will*: "The ideas and images in men's minds are the invisible powers that constantly govern them."[6] These thoughts should ultimately find their source in God.

In his letter to the Ephesians, Paul begins to unpack what types of things we are to dwell on, urging his readers to avoid being deceived by false teachings. Christians are to seek unity in the body of Christ by being one in faith and practice. But what does Paul mean by *unity*? Often this concept is misunderstood as ecumenical or interfaith unity. Paul, however, is calling us to something radically different. He is calling believers to Christian maturity, so that we are no longer like children who are "tossed to and fro by the waves and carried about by every wind of doctrine, by human cunning, by craftiness in deceitful schemes" (Ephesians 4:14). Paul makes a similar point to the Corinthian church in 2 Corinthians 11, warning believers not to be led astray from their pure devotion to Christ by "false apostles, deceitful workmen, disguising themselves as apostles of Christ" (verse 13).

Scripture calls us to "guard the good deposit entrusted to you" by the power of the Holy Spirit (2 Timothy 1:14). In his exhortation, Paul is concerned both with the *truth* with which God has entrusted us, as well as with the preservation of it in *faith* and *love*. Believers cannot accomplish this on their own, but rather by the power of the Holy Spirit. As Christians, a primary task is to guard the "good deposit."

One way to do this is by being equipped with the tools of discernment, so that we can approach theological texts with

---

6. Jonathan Edwards, *Freedom of the Will* (1754), www.ccel.org/ccel/edwards /will.iii.ix.html.

confidence and intentionality. We can then find worthy dialogue partners who can assist us in knowing God and ourselves better and being further equipped to live a life worthy of our calling in Christ. As pastor and homiletics professor Tony Merida correctly points out, our theology helps determine our biography. In other words, there is a direct correlation between what we believe and how we live our lives.[7] Therefore, it is vital that we consider who we allow to influence our theology. Scripture teaches this in Proverbs 13:20: "Whoever walks with the wise becomes wise, but the companion of fools will suffer harm." Let us choose, therefore, even in our reading, wise companions who will encourage us in our journey of faith. But how do we select these companions? Answering that question is part of the task of this book.

The following chapters will elaborate on *how* to train our minds and hearts to be more discerning readers of theology. The hope is that after reading this work, you will be better equipped to learn from those who have faithfully sought to know God and themselves according to God's revelation. A practical tool in this process is learning to ask the right kinds of questions of a theological work and knowing how to find the answers to them. These questions can be broken down into the following categories: the textual features, the context, the theological framework, the sources, the theologian's view, and assessing a work.

In the following chapters, we will cover each of these categories in greater depth, concluding with appendices on, among other things, how to practically share the tools of reading theology for all its worth in a classroom or discussion group.

---

7. Tony Merida, "The Essential Secret of Preaching," Desiring God, August 19, 2014, www.desiringgod.org/articles/the-essential-secret-of-preaching.

QUESTIONS FOR DISCUSSION AND REFLECTION

1. What do you see as the difference between knowledge and wisdom?
2. Tim Keller suggests that listening to hundreds of voices rather than just one will help you "become wise and develop your voice." Give one practical example of this from your life.
3. Paul warns believers not to be led astray from their pure devotion to Christ by "false apostles, deceitful workmen, disguising themselves as apostles of Christ" (2 Corinthians 11:13). What are some of the false teachings we need to beware of today?
4. What godly teachers have influenced you? What practical difference have they made in your life?
5. In what practical ways can you guard the "good deposit" given to you?
6. Tony Merida suggests that our theology helps determines our biography. Give an example of how you have seen this in your life or in the life of someone you admire.

CHAPTER 1

Overview: Getting Acquainted with the Tools of the Discerning Reader

Is not the great defect of our education today—a defect traceable through all the disquieting symptoms of trouble that I have mentioned—that although we often succeed in teaching our pupils "subjects," we fail lamentably on the whole in teaching them how to think: they learn everything, except the art of learning.

DOROTHY SAYERS,
"THE LOST TOOLS OF LEARNING"

Finally, brothers, whatever is true, whatever is honorable, whatever is just, whatever is pure, whatever is lovely, whatever is commendable, if there is any excellence, if there is anything worthy of praise, think about these things.

PHILIPPIANS 4:8

How do we discern wisdom? Judging intelligence is a far easier task than judging wisdom or divine truth. Yet Scripture calls us to do this very thing. It warns us that there are many false prophets in the world and in the church and calls to think about what is true and worthy of praise (Philippians 4:8; 2 Timothy 4:3–5; 1 John 4:1). One practical way to go about this task is by equipping ourselves with the tools of careful inspection.

WHAT IS THE MIND-SET OF A DISCERNING READER?

The task of knowing *who* to read and *how* to read theological works, for the Christian, is vital to learning *how* to interpret and apply the Word of God as part of the body of Christ.[1] The opposite can be true as well; knowing how to interpret and apply Scripture is vital to knowing *who* to read and *how* to read in theology. As the editors of a volume on theological methods point out, "Everyone interprets the Bible in their own way."[2] Whenever we come away from a Bible study or a sermon, we are well aware of the truth of this statement. Each reader has a lens or a bias by which he or she interprets both Scripture and the world. For example, the well-known verse John 3:16—"For God so loved the world that he gave his only Son, that whoever believes in him should not perish but have eternal life"—has been subject to vastly different interpretations. While

---

1. Both Dorothy Sayers, in *The Lost Tools of Learning* (paper read at a vacation course in education [London: Methuen, 1947]), and Mortimer Adler in *How to Read a Book* (New York: Simon & Schuster, 1972) recognize the vital importance of being equipped with the tools of learning. Neither, however, seeks to specifically train one to read with godly discernment, nor do they focus primarily on how to read theology.

2. Steven L. McKenzie and Stephen R. Haynes, eds., *To Each Its Own Meaning: An Introduction to Biblical Criticisms and Their Application*, rev. ed. (Louisville, KY: Westminster John Knox, 1999), 5.

the Arminian theologian (see the glossary if you are unfamiliar with this term or any others used in this text) would assert that this passage affirms that everybody has the opportunity to be saved, the Calvinist theologian would say this text teaches that only those who believe in Christ will be saved.[3] How can such a simple, well-known passage be understood in such radically different ways? The answer lies, in part, in what each reader of Scripture brings to the text.

It is beneficial, therefore, when approaching theological texts to be able to read between the lines, discerning the different perspectives, so that one can understand and evaluate the theology that is being taught. The author of Hebrews encourages this line of thinking: "Solid food is for the mature, for those who have their powers of discernment trained by constant practice to distinguish good from evil" (Hebrews 5:14). When equipped with the tools of careful inspection, a reader may glean the truths contained in the work and avoid believing that which leads us astray from Christ, as Paul warns about in Ephesians 4:1–16. This is particularly important for the young theologian, as Helmut Thielicke rightly suggests:

> My plea is simply this: every theological idea which makes an impression upon you must be regarded as a challenge to your faith. Do not assume as a matter of course that you believe whatever impresses you theologically and enlightens you intellectually. Otherwise suddenly you are believing no longer in Jesus Christ, but in Luther, or in one of your other theological teachers.[4]

One step in training our minds and hearts to be more discerning is learning *how* to listen well to a text, as we would listen to a

---

3. For example, see Reformed scholar R. C. Sproul's discussion ("John 3:16 and Man's Ability to Choose God," April 22, 2019, www.ligonier.org/blog /mans-ability-choose-god).

4. Helmut Thielicke, *A Little Exercise for Young Theologians* (Grand Rapids: Eerdmans, 1988), 59–60.

conversation partner.[5] Mortimer Adler, in his well-known classic *How to Read a Book*, suggests just this conversational approach:

> Reading a book should be a conversation between you and the author. Presumably he knows more about the subject than you do; if not, you probably should not be bothering with his book. But understanding is a two-way operation; the learner has to question himself and question the teacher. He even has to be willing to argue with the teacher, once he understands what the teacher is saying. Marking a book is literally an expression of your differences or your agreements. It is the highest respect you can pay him.[6]

Often we don't take the time to understand *what* the "teacher" is actually saying. Listening to a text is more than just reading the words on the page. It also requires understanding the author's perspective and his or her manner of communicating. As Deborah Tannen points out, "All communication is more or less cross-cultural. We learn to use language as we grow up, and growing up in different parts of the country, having different ethnic, religious, or class backgrounds, even just being male or female—all result in different ways of talking."[7] Add historical and presuppositional differences to this list, and it is understandable why truly perceiving what an author is saying can be such a challenging task.

5. Richard Langer of Biola University advocates for a conversational model for the integration of faith and learning (see, for example, Rick Langer, "Integration of Faith and Learning," https://cskls.org/wp-content/uploads/2019/06/Integration-of-Faith-and-Learning.pdf). His conversational model has implications not just for how we can approach other academic disciplines, but how we can approach texts that locate themselves within the Christian tradition. Similarly, Alan Jacobs endorses a conversational approach challenging his readers to approach texts by the "law of love," reading them "lovingly," just as we are called to love God and love neighbor (*A Theology of Reading: The Hermeneutics of Love* [Boulder, CO: Westview, 2001]).

6. Adler, *How to Read a Book*, 49.

7. Deborah Tannen, *That's Not What I Meant! How Conversational Style Makes or Breaks Relationships* (New York: Morrow, 1986), 10.

As Christians, however, we are called to wisdom, not to ignorance or a critical spirit. Scripture encourages us to be "quick to hear, slow to speak, slow to anger" (James 1:19). Furthermore, as Proverbs 1:5 (NIV) reads, "Let the wise listen and add to their learning, and let the discerning get guidance." Too often, we seek to be heard before we listen, and thus sow the seeds that foster what Deborah Tannen calls the "argument culture."[8] Rather than engaging in thoughtful, constructive dialogue, we can end up contributing to an adversarial culture either by erring on the side of "civility" or by manifesting a "warlike" mentality. We can seek to reverse this trend by training our minds and hearts to listen well to the Holy Spirit, as well as to the works with which we engage in conversation.

BECOMING A DISCERNING READER

A practical step to becoming a discerning reader who can recognize wisdom is learning to ask the right kinds of questions and knowing how to find the answers to those questions. These questions can be broken down into the following categories: the textual features, the context, the theological framework, the sources, the theologian's views, and assessing a work. In the following chapters, we will cover each of these categories in greater depth, but below is a broad overview of this process.

Textual Features and Publication Information
What do the textual features and publication information convey?
Much can be discovered about a theological text just by looking at the foreword, the introduction, the original publication date, the publisher, the table of contents, the footnotes/

---

8. Tannen writes, "The seeds of [the argument culture] can be found in our classrooms, where a teacher will introduce an article or an idea . . . setting up debates where people learn not to listen to each other because they're so busy trying to win the debate" (interview with David Gergen, "Argument Culture," *Newshour with Jim Lehrer*, March 27, 1988).

endnotes, and the bibliography. Examining publication information can help answer some of the following questions:

- **Who published the work?** Publishers gear their works to particular audiences and areas of interest.
- **When was the work originally published?** The original publication date can give you information about the context.
- **Who was the intended audience?** A theologian directs his or her work to a particular audience.
- **What was the purpose of the work?** Publishers and theologians have an aim behind the work.

The often neglected footnotes/endnotes and bibliography are also valuable resources for answering questions such as the following:

- **What types of sources does the theologian rely on?** Does the theologian cite primary or secondary sources? Are the sources secular or religious? Are they scientific, philosophical, or theological? Is Scripture a primary source? Each of these can impact the theologian's viewpoint.
- **What parts of Scripture does the theologian cite?** The parts of Scripture that the theologian primarily relies on—such as the Gospels, the Epistles, narrative texts, prophetic texts, wisdom literature, poetic texts—can impact his or her theological perspective.
- **Who has influenced the theologian?** Identify the specific theologians, thinkers, and schools of thought that the theologian favors.
- **With whom is the theologian dialoguing?** It is important to acknowledge whom the theologian seeks to support or refute.

We will look at these questions in more detail in chapter 3.

Context
What is the context of the work?

Context plays a crucial role in determining the meaning of a work. The context includes information not only about the setting of the text but also about the background of the theologian, whom the theologian is addressing, and the theologian's frame of reference. If we are to hear the theologian accurately, as he or she intends to be heard, we need to recognize the text's social, historical, and religious context and the intended goal of the text. Some of the questions we should address are the following:

- **What is the specific context of the work?** This includes examining the sociopolitical and ecclesiastical context of the theological work.
- **Why did the theologian write the work?** Examine the explicit and implicit motives and goals of the theologian.
- **What is the theologian's background?** This includes the theologian's religious/denominational background, educational training, ethnic background, and sociopolitical background.
- **What is the theologian's frame of reference? What type of theologian is he or she?** A theologian can speak as a biblical, systematic, historical, practical, moral, philosophical, ideological, or apologetic theologian.
- **What is the theologian's role?** A theologian can write from the position of a narrator, pastor, scientist, philosopher, teacher, or historian.
- **What are the theologian's presuppositions?** A theologian's presuppositions include his or her views about who God is, what is authoritative, who we are and where we came from, what the problem is that needs to be resolved, and what the remedy is.

Chapter 4 will further discuss these vital questions.

The Theological Framework
What is the theological framework of the work?

The discerning reader should be able to identify the topic of the work, the type of work, and the approach the theologian uses to express his or her theological views. These pieces of information help unpack the meaning of the text.

- **What is the topic of the work?** Identify whether the topic is the method of theology, the doctrine of revelation, God, Christ, Holy Spirit, creation, humanity, the fall and sin, salvation, the church, the Christian life, or the future.
- **What type of theological work is it?** Identify whether it is a sermon, a theological treatise, a polemic, a response, a creed, a confession, a catechism, a commentary, a theological reference work, a systematic work, a satire, a story, a poem, a hymn, a memoir, an apologetic work, a mystical work, or a devotional work.
- **What theological approach does the author utilize?** Identify whether the approach is propositional, experiential, systemic, historical, praxis, neoorthodox, postliberal, postconservative, or correlational.

We will explore these topics in more depth in chapter 5.

The Sources
How does the theologian utilize sources?

Part of the task of discerning the framework includes identifying the sources. It is essential to identify not only *what* sources the theologian uses but also *how* the theologian utilizes them.

- **What types of sources does the theologian utilize?** Identify the theologian's reliance on reason, tradition, science, philosophy, Scripture, and personal experience.

- **What sources does the theologian prioritize?** How much weight does the author give to the sources used? Is one favored over others? Is one source heavily refuted?
- **How does the theologian interact with the sources?** Does he or she use them to support his or her position, to argue against other positions, for the purpose of illustration, and so forth.

These questions will be elaborated on in chapter 6.

The Theologian's Viewpoint
What are the theologian's views?

The heart of dialoguing with anyone is being able to actively listen and grasp what is really important to that person. To be a good conversation partner with a theological text, one must be able to consider the author's viewpoint. This dialogue becomes possible once the reader can identify the following: the thesis, the main arguments, and the key terms the theologian utilizes.

- **What are the thesis and key points?** Restate the thesis and key ideas in your own words.
- **What are the key terms that are important to the theologian's arguments?** Define the words that are unfamiliar or are vital to the key ideas.

These questions will be unpacked in chapter 7.

Assessing the Work
What is the value of the work?

Once the hard work of careful inspection is done, the reader is ready to critically and appreciatively evaluate the work. The value of a theological work does not merely rest in how readable it is or how closely it aligns with one's own beliefs, but in how it moves one toward knowing and loving God and loving others (Matthew 22:36–40). Sometimes the work points us toward truth; sometimes it helps point out flaws in our thinking; sometimes it makes us aware of the dangers of holding unbiblical beliefs. Other times the work clarifies important concepts or terms, helps us understand doctrinal developments in the history of the church, or defends a key orthodox doctrine.

- **Pray for discernment.** Ask the Holy Spirit to give you discernment in recognizing and applying God's truth.
- **Steep yourself in God's Word.** Consider what God's Word communicates about the topic or ideas in the theological text.
- **Test and evaluate the text against Scripture.** Evaluate the biblical accuracy of the theologian's ideas.
- **Discover the value and implications of the text.** Identify what the text teaches about God, ourselves, and the world. Think about the implications of this work for Christianity and society.
- **Ask probing questions.** Did the work help me understand a position, viewpoint, or movement I wasn't familiar with before? Did it deepen my knowledge of the historical or contemporary circumstances of the church? Did it broaden my horizons? Did it challenge me to clarify or defend my own position?

This final category will be more fully covered in chapter 8.

CONCLUSION

Alexander Pope's famous proverbial saying—"fools rush in where angels fear to tread"[9]—cautions us against rashly attempting something that a more experienced person would avoid. Yet we

---

9. Alexander Pope, *An Essay on Criticism, 1711* (London: Lewis, 1711), 36.

constantly do just that when we analyze and apply the ideas of a theological work before taking the time to carefully examine the text. From the moment we pick up a book, we begin to form opinions about its value. The full assessment of a theological work, however, should ideally happen after a careful inspection of it in order to avoid hasty, unfounded judgments, whether they be positive or negative. To assess a work after a simple first reading would be similar to judging a person based on a first impression.

In his book *Blink*, Malcolm Gladwell investigates how decisions are made in an instant, some good and some bad. He recounts the story of a statue that the Getty Museum had procured that was later discovered to be a forgery. However, many experts' initial impressions suggested it was a genuine Greek *kouros* (statue of a standing nude youth). Gladwell's story points out the power of first impressions.

While first impressions are important, they can be misguided. Our instincts can properly direct us or betray us. Gladwell rightly argues, however, that "our snap judgments and first impressions can be educated and controlled."[10] The same can be said for judgments of theological works. If we bring a well-trained mind into the reading process, we are apt to learn considerably more when we choose to dialogue thoughtfully and carefully with the author, whether or not we end up agreeing. As Christians, however, we are called to train not only our minds to discern truth, but also our hearts, learning to listen to and obey the Holy Spirit (Romans 8:14).

The following chapters will further explore how to read theology for all its worth. After reading this book, I hope you will be more prepared to discern the valuable insights in theological works, being equipped to learn from those who have faithfully sought to know God and themselves according to God's revelation.

---

10. Malcolm Gladwell, *Blink: The Power of Thinking without Thinking* (New York: Little, Brown, 2005), 15.

QUESTIONS FOR DISCUSSION AND REFLECTION

1. What books have had the most significant impact on your life and why?
2. How do you go about choosing the books you read? Do you see books as teachers, peers, sparring partners, or something else? What type of book makes the best conversation partner for you? Why?
3. What is the first thing you usually do when you're reading a book? How does this impact how much you get out of the book?
4. If you were a book, what kind of takeaways would you want your readers to have? How could this inform the way you read?
5. Helmut Thielicke states that the "very theological idea which makes an impression upon you must be regarded as a challenge to your faith. Do not assume as a matter of course that you believe whatever impresses you theologically and enlightens you intellectually. Otherwise suddenly you are believing no longer in Jesus Christ, but in Luther, or in one of your other theological teachers." Define the purpose of reading theology. How should we view the theologians we read?

PRACTICE GETTING ACQUAINTED WITH THE TOOLS OF DISCERNMENT

What are the tools for careful inspection?

1. Identify three steps you can start utilizing in your reading of theology that will enable you to get more out of the works you are reading.
2. How can you implement these steps with the next theological text you read?
3. Implement at least one of them and describe its impact on your understanding of this theological text.

CHAPTER 2

Preparing for Reading Theology for All Its Worth: Being Steeped in Prayer and Scripture

The Christian leaders of the future have to be theologians, persons who know the heart of God and are trained—through prayer, study, and careful analysis—to manifest the divine event of God's saving work in the midst of the many seemingly random events of their time.

HENRI NOUWEN, *IN THE NAME OF JESUS*

How blessed is the man who does not walk in the counsel of
   the wicked,
Nor stand in the path of sinners,
Nor sit in the seat of scoffers!
But his delight is in the law of the LORD,
And in His law he meditates day and night.
He will be like a tree firmly planted by streams of water,
Which yields its fruit in its season
And its leaf does not wither;
And in whatever he does, he prospers.

PSALM 1:1–3 NASB

HOW DO YOU PREPARE YOURSELF
TO READ THEOLOGY?

Being steeped in prayer and Scripture are essential to Christian discernment and spiritual flourishing. Imagine a farmer going out to harvest a crop, having neglected to prepare the soil and plant the seeds. What should the farmer expect to find? At best, some leftover yield from past harvests or a volunteer crop that had not been intentionally planted. We, like the farmer, need to prepare our hearts and minds if we intend to have discernment, spiritual prosperity, and spiritual fruit.

Psalm 1:1–3 (NASB) gives us a picture of the benefits of meditating on God's Word:

> How blessed is the man who does not walk in the
>   counsel of the wicked,
> Nor stand in the path of sinners,
> Nor sit in the seat of scoffers!
> But his delight is in the law of the LORD,
> And in His law he meditates day and night.
> He will be like a tree firmly planted by streams of water,
> Which yields its fruit in its season
> And its leaf does not wither;
> And in whatever he does, he prospers.

Similarly, the psalmist cries out to God in prayer for discernment in Psalm 119:125: "I am your servant; give me understanding, that I may know your testimonies!"

Being steeped in prayer and Scripture is vital for a Christian. Recognizing this, Henri Nouwen calls us to be theologians "who know the heart of God and are trained—through prayer, study, and careful analysis—to manifest the divine event of

God's saving work in the midst of the many seemingly random events of their time."[1] Prayer and deep study of Scripture are essential to reading theology for all its worth.

CHRISTIAN THEOLOGY AND PRAYER

What is the relationship between prayer and theology?

Prayer should be a part of the whole reading process, particularly in discerning how to apply a theological work to one's life. Prayer and Christian theology are inseparable if we want to avoid being theologians who are primarily interested in speculative academic debates that have little relevance to increasing our knowledge of God or of ourselves. Prayer acknowledges our dependence on God for knowing the truth and living it out. The practice of prayer invites God into the discernment process.

As the word *theology* suggests (*theos* meaning "God," and *logos* meaning "word" or "study of"), the Christian theologian is called to know God according to God's self-revelation. Christian theology is, however, as Dennis Okholm asserts, a very human activity. It is "a (a) *human* (b) *response to the revelation of God*, done (c) *within and for the Christian church*, which engages in (d) *critical reflection for responsible talk* about God."[2]

If it is to be more than human philosophy, Christian theology requires faith that is rooted in prayer and in the conviction that God inspired the biblical writers (1 Corinthians 2:13; 2 Timothy 3:16; 2 Peter 1:20–21). While it recognizes that Scripture does not reveal everything about God, Christian theology acknowledges that God's Word is sufficient for salvation and for our needs (2 Peter 1:3). Good theology points to the living God to find the

---

1. Henri Nouwen, *In the Name of Jesus: Reflections on Christian Leadership* (New York: Crossroad, 1989), 88.

2. Dennis Okholm, *Learning Theology through the Church's Worship: An Introduction to Christian Belief* (Grand Rapids: Baker Academic, 2018), 25, italics original.

ultimate truths about God, ourselves, and the world. It finds its source in the Word and prayer and is done in service of the church. Jesus Christ, the living Word (John 1:1, 14; Revelation 19:13), and God's written revelation in Scripture (2 Timothy 3:16) are the ultimate starting points of Christian theology.

The study of theology is a communal event and is not to be done in isolation. Its aim is both personal and relational, helping us understand our need for reconciliation with God and neighbor and building us into the body of Christ (Ephesians 2:16–22). Therefore, theology's ultimate goal is not merely knowledge; instead, it is a personal and communal knowledge of God that leads to a life of worship of the living God. Prayer helps theology achieve this divine end.

As noted above, there is a deep connection between prayer and theology. How we speak about God and how we speak to God are inextricably linked. Our private prayers are excellent indicators of our true theology. If we truly believe we are sinful and are dependent on Christ for life, knowledge, and salvation, then our prayers will reflect that. Likewise, our theology informs our prayers. As we grow in our knowledge of God and of ourselves, our praise of God is deeply enriched.

This is reflected in David's prayer in Psalm 51 after the prophet Nathan confronted him. Based on God's love and compassion, David pleads for God's mercy after being convicted of his sins of adultery and murder. David knows he is sinful and does not deserve forgiveness, but he still cries out to God to wash away his iniquity and renew him. David's theology, his knowledge of his depravity and God's righteousness and mercy, inform his prayer. His prayer, in turn, helps shape his relationship with God. We, like David, need to depend on God to convict us of our sins, reveal our blind spots, and instruct us in true wisdom (Psalm 51:6).

Similarly, when we are reading and assessing theology, we need to seek God's wise counsel. When we enter into a posture of prayer, we prepare ourselves to discern God's truth. In prayer, we have the opportunity to recognize God's greatness and our need for God's revelation and intervention in our lives. Prayer keeps our pride in check and opens our hearts and minds to hearing and responding to God's truth by the power of the Holy Spirit. As C. S. Lewis points out, pride separates us from proper communion with God and others:

> In God you come up against something which is in every respect immeasurably superior to yourself. Unless you know God as that—and, therefore, know yourself as nothing in comparison—you do not know God at all. As long as you are proud you cannot know God. A proud man is always looking down on things and people: and, of course, as long as you are looking down, you cannot see something that is above you.[3]

In light of the purpose of theology, we should not read and assess works simply to identify what is wrong or lacking, or even to build up our intellectual knowledge. Rather, we should appraise these works so that we may know whether they can be of assistance in properly knowing and loving God and others.

When praying through the reading process, seek to be honest with God, wherever you currently are, opening space to allow the Holy Spirit to speak to you. Pray for the Spirit's guidance in knowing God's truths and how to walk in them (Psalm 86:11). Ask the Spirit to guide your thoughts and feelings, revealing where you or the theologian you are dialoguing with may be right or wrong. Scripture encourages believers to fellowship and to seek to sharpen one another, to make us more effective servants of the Lord (Proverbs 27:17; Colossians 3:16; Hebrews 3:13). Pray that in your dialogue with theological texts, you may be sanctified.

---

3. C. S. Lewis, *Mere Christianity* (1943; repr., New York: Macmillan, 1960), 111.

Below are some helpful insights about prayer from Scripture that you can keep in mind when reading a theological work:

- God promises to reveal great and unsearchable things in the Word (Jeremiah 33:3).
- You are called to devote yourself to prayer, being watchful and thankful (Colossians 4:2).
- You are called to pray with thanksgiving and ask for wisdom and discernment (Philippians 4:6–7).
- God promises to be near, hear your cries, and provide help, mercy, and grace in times of need (Psalm 18:6; Jeremiah 29:13; Hebrews 4:16; 1 John 5:14).
- You are called to confess your sins and pray for others, including those who mistreat you (Luke 6:27–28; James 5:16).
- You are called to watch and pray so that you will not fall into temptation and will know the will of God (Jeremiah 42:3; Colossians 1:9; Matthew 6:9–13).
- The Spirit promises to help you in your weakness, interceding for you in prayer (Romans 8:26).

Praying in accordance with Scripture will help reveal what you should believe about who God is, who you are, and what God has done. Prayer will also help you keep your priorities in line with God's by revealing your own biases, desires, and misdirected aims. Ultimately, it will keep your theology from being merely speculative by directing you to the worship of the triune God.

BEING STEEPED IN SCRIPTURE
What does God's Word communicate?

We should begin reading theology, as Solomon did in 1 Kings 3:9, with prayer, recognizing our fallenness and asking God to give us an "understanding mind" so that we "may discern between good and evil." Then, as Tim Challies suggests, we should make a "deliberate effort" to distinguish "between what is true and what is false"[4] We can seek to do this by prayerfully reading, testing, and evaluating the text against the Word of God, the ultimate source of truth, and discovering its implications.

Just as bank tellers learn how to recognize counterfeit bills by studying real money, readers of theology should learn to recognize heresy (false teachings) by studying the Word of God. Students of theology should be steeped in prayer and Scripture so that when they read theology, they can discern God's truth. As Hebrews 4:12 declares, "The word of God is living and active, sharper than any two-edged sword, piercing to the division of soul and of spirit, of joints and of marrow, and discerning the thoughts and intentions of the heart."

This principle can work in two directions, helping readers of theology to discern the state of their own hearts and beliefs, as well as those of the theologian. Often we approach a theological work or even Scripture with preconceived notions that inhibit us from seeing anything but what we expect to see. When one is steeped in prayer and Scripture, one opens the door to the conviction of the Holy Spirit and to God's voice (1 Corinthians 2:14–16; Ephesians 1:17–18).

When you prayerfully examine Scripture, it is helpful to have the following questions in mind:

- **What is the genre of the text?** Recognize if the genre is narrative, prophetic, poetic, historical, a gospel, or an epistle and think about how it might affect the message.
- **What is the context of the passage?** This includes the historical, cultural, literary, specific, and broader biblical context of the passage.

---

4. Tim Challies, *The Discipline of Spiritual Discernment* (Wheaton, IL: Crossway, 2007), 67.

- **What is the author's original purpose?** Identify the author's original intent in writing.
- **What are the key theological themes and ideas communicated in the text?** Look for what theological truths it reveals about God, Christ, the Holy Spirit, the cosmos, humans, sin, salvation, Scripture, Israel, the church, and the future. In Christian theology, it is important to have a Christ-centered approach, focusing first on what the passage reveals about God and the gospel.
- **What is the plain or obvious meaning of the passage?** Seek to interpret passages according to the obvious meaning, unless the literary context clearly leads you to interpret it in another manner, such as by means of metaphors or ironic sayings.
- **How does the Bible interpret itself?** Carefully compare related passages to help shed light on what the passage means.
- **What are the timeless principles of the passage?** Recognize what truths the Holy Spirit is communicating to all people.

This short list will help guide your reading of Scripture. There are many helpful books to further train you in how to read the Bible. For instance, Gordon Fee and Douglas Stuart's *How to Read the Bible for All Its Worth* and Howard and William Hendricks's *Living by the Book* are great introductory books. Trent Hunter and Stephen Wellum's *Christ from Beginning to End* is helpful in training the reader to understand the significance of the context of Scripture. These are wonderful resources to deepen your understanding of Scripture.[5] To

---

5. Gordon D. Fee and Douglas Stuart, *How to Read the Bible for All Its Worth*, 4th ed. (Grand Rapids: Zondervan, 2014); William Hendricks, *Living by the Book: The Art and Science of Reading the Bible*, rev. ed. (Chicago: Moody, 2007); Trent Hunter and Stephen Wellum, *Christ from Beginning to End:*

develop your biblical discernment, it is important to prayerfully steep yourself in God's Word, asking the Spirit for insight. John 17:17 (NIV) declares the transforming power of prayer and God's Word: "Sanctify them by the truth; your word is truth."

CONCLUSION

Ad fontes—"back to the fountain," or "back to the original sources"—was one of the rallying cries of the Reformation. This phrase occurs in the Latin Vulgate's version of Psalm 42, which can be translated "in the same way that the stag is drawn unto the sources of water, so my soul is drawn unto you, God." Thirsting for God's truth, Protestant Reformers went back to the Bible, prayerfully studying it in its original languages. We too should desire to know God and commune with him, seeking enlightenment in prayerfully considering his Word. Do not wait until you are fully trained to devote yourself to prayer and the study of Scripture. A strong biblical foundation is one of the best ways to prepare for discerning God's wisdom and will. It is also essential to reading theological texts for all their worth.

QUESTIONS FOR DISCUSSION AND REFLECTION

1. Scripture highlights the importance of spending time in prayer and God's Word. Give a few practical benefits of engaging in these practices.
2. Henri Nouwen writes, "The Christian leaders of the future have to be theologians, persons who know the heart of God and are trained—through prayer, study, and careful analysis—to manifest the divine event of God's saving work in the midst of the many

---

How the Full Story of Scripture Reveals the Full Glory of Christ (Grand Rapids: Zondervan, 2018).

seemingly random events of their time." What are some of the seemingly random events of our day? How do prayer and the study of Scripture help us manifest the gospel amidst them?

3. Dennis Okholm asserts that Christian theology is a very human activity. It is "a human response to the revelation of God, done within and for the Christian church, which engages in critical reflection for responsible talk about God." How does this statement impact your view of the theological texts you read?

4. How we speak *about* God and how we speak *to* God are inextricably linked. Give a practical example of how our theology can impact our prayer lives.

5. How can David's prayer in Psalm 51 guide you in your prayers? In your reading of theology?

6. Look at the list of insights about prayer from Scripture. Which one speaks most to you right now? Why?

7. We often approach a theological work or even Scripture with preconceived notions or biases that inhibit us from seeing anything but what we expect to see. Give an example of a preconceived notion or bias that you have seen impact a person's understanding of a theological work or Scripture.

8. Look at Psalm 1 with the questions listed under "Being Steeped in Scripture." Give three insights based on these questions.

PRACTICE BEING STEEPED IN PRAYER AND SCRIPTURE

How do you prepare yourself to read theology?

1. Spending time in prayer and Scripture is vital to the Christian. Spend some time prayerfully meditating on Psalm 1. Record at least one insight you gained from your time.

2. How could this passage impact the way you approach reading Scripture? Theology?

3. Implement this insight and describe the impact it had on you.

CHAPTER 3

First Steps: Examining Textual Features and Publication Information

Why, it's one o' the books I bought at Partridge's sale. They was all bound alike—it's a good binding, you see—and I thought they'd be all good books . . . But it seems one mustn't judge by th' outside.

GEORGE ELIOT, *THE MILL ON THE FLOSS*

Do not judge by appearances, but judge with right judgment.

JOHN 7:24

Remember the adage "Don't judge a book by its cover." In George Eliot's novel, *The Mill on the Floss*, Mr. Tulliver defends his decision to buy a well-bound but questionable book for his daughter. He laments, "Why, it's one o' the books I bought at Partridge's sale. They was all bound alike—it's a good binding, you see—and I thought they'd be all good books . . . But it seems one mustn't judge by th' outside."[1] The message behind the cliché is good and even biblical: we should not form an opinion *solely* based on superficial observations.

In John 7:24, Jesus urges his listeners not to judge based only on appearances, but to exercise "right judgment." He teaches that godly judgment must be based on truth, not just on first impressions or prejudice. This does not mean, however, that the outside of a book does not have any significance, as the cliché seems to suggest. Valuable information can and should be gleaned from the cover and other textual features of a book. A well-trained mind can, in fact, make some important initial observations or judgments about a book based on its cover.

As soon as you look at a book, whether you know it or not, you begin to assess it. The design of the cover; the title; the associations you have with the author, publisher, and those who endorse the book; the length and the font of the text all influence your perceptions of it. Within the first few seconds of examining this book, for instance, you made a number of judgments. What is this book about? Is the topic valuable for you? Do you respect the author and the publisher? Does it look interesting? Is it easy to read? Is it worth the cost? Some of your judgments of this book happened before you even read a single page. It's important to recognize that it is not wrong to judge

---

1. George Eliot, *The Mill on the Floss*, vol. 1 (Edinburgh: Blackwood, 1878), 22.

a book and its teachings, but rather essential. We are called to seek true knowledge (Proverbs 18:5; Matthew 7:15–20; Titus 1:6–16; 2 Peter 2). The real issue is whether or not we have "right" judgments, even regarding our initial impressions. Training can help us make "right" judgments.

So where should you begin to accurately assess a theological work? For example, say you are assigned to choose the next theological text for your book club, Bible study, or class. How do you decide what your group will read? You could search the internet for a list of works, but you would probably still have a large number of books from which to choose. Rather than taking the time to read every work listed, you can save a lot of effort by beginning your evaluation with the cover and other textual features. You can discover a lot about a theological text by examining the title, author information, original publication date, publisher, endorsements, foreword, introduction, table of contents, footnotes/endnotes, bibliography, and other additional features.

BEGINNING WITH THE COVER AND PUBLICATION INFORMATION

What do the textual features and publication information convey?

Examining the cover and the publication information is a vital component in introducing yourself to a text. Even the artwork can give you initial information about the work. For example, if you look up the title *Don't Judge a Book by Its Cover*, you will find no less than half a dozen books with that title. Which one do you choose?

The one by Robbie Michaels pictures a young man on the cover and is a romance novel geared toward young adults, whereas the same title by Josh Benya has an alligator on the cover and is a children's book. If you are looking for an academic book about the significance of book covers, you could quickly eliminate these two books in favor of Nicole Matthews and Nickianne Moody's work titled *Judging a Book by Its Cover*. The subtitle—*Fans, Publishers, Designers, and the Marketing of Fiction*—and the cover design, with a large printed title and two older fiction book images, help the potential reader recognize that this work is intended to explain the significance of fiction book covers.

Publishers use the book cover to introduce a book to a potential reader. It serves as the "face" of the book and helps generate expectations about what is inside, just as a smile or a frown generates expectations of the mood of a person. Spending a few minutes examining the book cover and publication information, including the table of contents, can help you answer some of the following essential questions, which we will unpack in the rest of this chapter:

- What is the significance of the title of the work?
- Who wrote the work?
- Who published the work?
- When was the work originally written and published?
- Is it a translation?
- What edition is it?
- Who is the intended audience?
- What is the purpose of the work?
- Who has endorsed the work?
- What topics are covered in the table of contents?

What Is the Significance of the Title of the Work?

When examining a work, generally the title is the first thing you read. The title communicates the essence of the book and markets it to the target audience. The title and subtitle, supplied either by the author or the publisher, should serve as a concise summary of the book. For example, *Confessions of Saint Augustine* is a spiritual memoir, whereas *The City of God against the Pagans* is Augustine's theology of history and society. The two titles help indicate the different aims of the works: one is focused on Augustine's life, and the other is focused on the world. If the title is initially unclear or obscure, such as *Institutes of Elenctic Theology* by Francis Turretin, it may signal that it is intended for a specific target audience. Elenctic theology is a debate-style format whereby the author not only sets out what is true but refutes what is false. This work was written in the seventeenth century for Reformed students at the academy in Geneva not only to establish the Reformed position but also to refute Catholic theology.

Subtitles typically help contextualize a work by illuminating the central premise, audience, and goal. Elisabeth Schüssler Fiorenza's work *In Memory of Her: A Feminist Theological Reconstruction of Christian Origins* is a good example. The subtitle lets the reader know that she is writing from a feminist perspective to empower women by bringing to light the role that women have played in the origins of Christianity. Without the subtitle, the title is very vague and the work could be mistaken as a biography.

Who Wrote the Work?

Often the back cover or the inside of the cover will give a brief introduction to the author, including his or her credentials, religious/scholarly affiliations, and other works the author has published. This initial biographical information will help establish the credibility of the author. Is the author affiliated with a reputable academic or ecclesiastical institution? Does the author have a particular expertise or training? What is the author known for? For instance, from the back cover of the book *The Triune God*, we can learn that the author, Fred Sanders, received his PhD from Graduate Theological Union, Berkeley, and that he is a professor of theology in the Torrey Honors Institute at Biola University. He also has published a number of books about the Trinity, including *The Deep Things of God: How the Trinity Changes Everything*, and he is a popular blogger at *Scriptorium Daily*. If you wanted to discover more information about Sanders, the biographical information given on the cover points you to both Biola and his blog.

Who Published the Work?

Publishers have different concerns and gear their works to particular audiences and areas of interest. It is important to recognize, for instance, if the publisher is secular or religious. A secular publisher tends to publish works geared toward mainstream or secular academic audiences, whereas religious publishers tend to focus on a narrower readership. Some religious publishing houses may be owned by a secular company, such as in the case of Christian publisher Zondervan, which was acquired by HarperCollins in 1988. HarperCollins owns around fifty imprints, including Harlequin Enterprises and HarperTeen. Each of these publishing arms has a different target audience.

It is helpful to discern the affiliation of religious publishers. Is the publisher Catholic, Evangelical, Lutheran, Reformed, Eastern Orthodox, or some other association? Catholic publisher Emmaus Academic markets itself as the academic arm of the St. Paul Center for Biblical Theology, whereas Augsburg Fortress is the publishing house of the Evangelical Lutheran Church in America. These two different affiliations impact what works the publishers print. The mission of Emmaus is "to participate in the renewal of Catholic theology through publishing the very best in faithful scholarship."[2] In contrast, "Augsburg Fortress develops engaging resources for Lutheran congregations."[3] It is important to recognize that these publishers are seeking to promote a Catholic or Lutheran perspective.

---

2. "Our Mission," Emmaus Academic, www.emmausacademic.com/about.
3. "About Us," Augsburg Fortress, www.augsburgfortress.org/info/about.jsp.

Other important questions to ask about the publisher are whether they gear their publications primarily toward an academic or a popular audience, and if the publishing house has a specialty. For instance, Eric Metaxas's biography, *Martin Luther: The Man Who Rediscovered God and Changed the World*, is published by the popular publishing house Viking and is geared toward a mainstream audience, whereas Martin Brecht's benchmark three-volume work on Luther is published by Fortress Press for an academic audience. Some publishers may specialize in publishing monographs, textbooks, Bible studies, commentaries, historical works, contemporary works, or even self-help books.

A final question to ask is, What is the publisher's reputation? This is particularly important with the rise in self-publishing and blogs that allow anyone to be a "published" author. While these writings can be valuable resources, reputable publishing houses, where well-known theologians are published, lend credibility to a work. Reputable publishers generally vet the books they publish and provide editorial input and peer reviews to the authors.

Some publishers give very little guidance to their authors and are basically the equivalent of self-publishing. If the work is a monograph, a lesser-known publisher may be legitimate, particularly if the work has already gone through a rigorous editing process. This is often the case with published dissertations. In these situations, however, it may be helpful to look at some book reviews to get a better understanding of the value of a work.

When Was the Work Originally Written and Published?

The original writing and publication date can give you some initial information about the context and purpose of a theological work. How one dates a theological work can affect how it is interpreted. A common mistake is to assume that the publication date is the same as when the work was written. For example, how are we to date Athanasius's work *On the Incarnation*? Let's say the edition you're reading gives the publication date of 1981 and lists C. S. Lewis as the author of the introduction. It is evident that 1981 cannot be the date that the work was written or originally published, since both Athanasius and Lewis were deceased by 1981 (Athanasius passed away in 373 and Lewis in 1963). So when was it actually written? Was it before or after the first Council of Nicaea? Before or after Athanasius became the bishop of Alexandria? Was he refuting Arian heresy (which denied the divinity of Christ), summarizing Nicene orthodoxy (which defined Christ's relationship to the Trinity), or writing it prior to either of these? Discovering the year the work was written helps the reader determine Athanasius's purpose in writing.

Is It a Translation?

It is important to note whether or not a work is a translation. Translations can add another interpretative layer to understanding a theological work. Think, for example, about the differences between Bible translations. Most readers cannot read the Bible in its original languages, so translations are vital. But why do we have so many different English translations? This reality is a result of several factors: the recognition that the English language is always changing; the reliance of translators on different manuscripts; and the various approaches used in Bible translation. A good translation, as C. S. Lewis mentions in his introduction to the modern English translation of Athanasius's *On the Incarnation*, makes a work more accessible to the average reader.[4]

---

4. Athanasius, *On the Incarnation: The Treatise De Incarnatione Verbi Dei*, trans. Penelope Lawson, intro. by C. S. Lewis (New York: Macmillan, 1981), xv.

If you cannot read a work in its original language, it is vital to seek out a translation that accurately and effectively conveys not only the author's words but also his or her ideas. If you are having trouble unpacking a particular word, phrase, or idea, it can be helpful to see if there is more than one translation of that work. For example, Martin Luther uses the German term *Anfechtung* when he is describing his life before his conversion. This term does not have a precise English equivalent. If you look it up in a German dictionary, you will find it defined as "contesting," "challenging," "avoiding," "attack," "trial," or "tribulation." You will find that one translator of Luther uses "temptation," another "trials," and a third "affliction." The American translation of *Luther's Works*, a reputable translation, chooses to use all three and adds "tribulation." Each of these translations helps unpack this obscure, multifaceted term. Poor or archaic translations can further obscure the meaning of the text.

What Edition Is It?

Be sure to pay attention to whether the work is a first edition or a later edition. This information hints at whether this work has been popular, has possibly been revised, and has stood the test of time. Generally, it is best to choose the most recent edition. For example, the third edition of the *Evangelical Dictionary of Theology* includes new articles and revisions to make it relevant to contemporary audiences.

There are, however, exceptions to this rule of thumb. For instance, earlier editions may be geared toward a different audience or may be helpful in accessing an author's earlier thought. Such is the case with John Calvin's *Institutes of the Christian Religion*. The value of each edition of the *Institutes* is in part dependent on your purpose for reading it. If you are looking for an early work directed toward the religious education of Protestants, then the first edition published in 1536 would be of interest. If, however, you are looking for a more developed systematic work written during the Reformation, you would prefer to examine the fifth edition, published in 1559. If you want to read the standard English translation, you would probably look at the 1960 edition translated by Ford Lewis Battles and edited by John T. McNeill. Versions can vary significantly in content, format, language, and resources.

Who Is the Intended Audience?

An author and a publisher generally direct a work to a particular audience. Is it aimed at a like-minded audience or one that stands in opposition to the author's ideas? A secular or religious audience? An academic or popular audience? Novices or experts? A specific discipline—such as psychology, sociology, church history, the sciences, the humanities? A particular group—youth, women, men, high schoolers, college students, seminarians, a denomination, a particular faith, or ethnic group? For example, C. S. Lewis's *The Abolition of Man*, subtitled *Reflections on Education with Special Reference to the Teaching of English in the Upper Forms of Schools*, was initially given as a series of lectures in 1943 at the University of Durham during World War II as a critique of the modern understanding of values. This work was directed to an audience of academics, particularly those in the area of teaching English. *That Hideous Strength: A Modern Fairy-Tale for Grown-Ups*, which was published in 1945, is a novelization of *The Abolition of Man*. Lewis wrote this literary work to convey his criticism of modernity to a broader audience. While both works share similar philosophical and theological insights, they differ in their format and intended audience. The book's subtitle, cover description, and table of contents help identify the specific intended audience of each work.

What Is the Purpose of the Work?

As previously mentioned, publishers and authors have an aim behind the work. Discovering the purpose, however, can take a bit of detective work. Generally, the title, description, table of contents, and introduction convey the author's intent. Is it to tell a story, describe an idea, inform, instruct, train, entertain, or convince the reader to believe something? For example, Evangelical apologist J. P. Moreland's purpose in writing *The God Conversation: Using Stories and Illustrations to Explain Your Faith* is to equip Christians about how to converse well with people about their faith. On the other hand, Moreland's book *The God Question: An Invitation to a Life of Meaning* is directed to thoughtful non-Christians who are open to learning about the Christian life, as well as to Christians who want more from their faith than just "being religious." Both works discuss profound questions about God and faith, but one is focused on equipping the believer and one is focused on answering the questions of the seeker or questioning Christian. The different purposes impact the content of the message and the manner in which it is delivered.

Who Has Endorsed the Work?

The back and inside covers often include endorsements. Glancing over these can help you determine whether you want to read the book. Endorsements provide brief statements about the value of the work, the content, and the style. Generally, the more well-known, influential endorsers are listed first. It is helpful to ask if the work is endorsed by an expert on the subject and what the endorser values about the work. Publishers know that endorsements are one of the most important features for marketing a book. Respected experts in the field generally write helpful endorsements that give you a sense of the worth of the book.

Endorsements can be particularly helpful when you are evaluating a newer work or something by a relatively unknown author. If you are interested in the topic of the theology of singleness, for example, you may come across the book by Christina Hitchcock titled *The Significance of Singleness: A Theological*

Vision for the Future of the Church. There are a number of endorsements to help you discern if this book will be valuable for you, including ones written by Steven Garber (Regent College), Ian A. McFarland (University of Cambridge), Lisa Graham McMinn (George Fox University), Jason Byassee (Vancouver School of Theology), Kimlyn J. Bender (Baylor University), and David Rylaarsdam (Calvin Theological Seminary).

The scholars endorsing the book are experts in leadership, anthropology, sociology, gender, biblical interpretation, ethics, and spiritual formation. Garber's endorsement reveals that it is both a theological and personal book that is historically situated in church history while also being attentive to "contemporary complexities of sexuality, marriage, and family." It is geared for those who are dealing with the tension of being holy and human in the modern world. McFarland's endorsement helps the reader recognize that Hitchcock's work is written from a distinctly Evangelical perspective that is relevant to non-Evangelicals as well.

These endorsements are helpful in giving concise summaries of the type of audience that may appreciate this work, the relevant topics included, the writing style of the author, and its contribution to the field of current gender issues in the church. All of this information is helpful in becoming familiar with the work.

What Topics Are Covered in the Table of Contents?

The table of contents is like a map that the publisher has provided to help you navigate your way through the book. Examining the table of contents, just like looking at a road map, can point out where the author is going and how they plan to get there. A well-written table of contents identifies the major ideas and possibly sub-ideas of each chapter or section and directs you to where to find them.

Other additional material at the front or back of the book, such as the foreword, dedication, and epigraph, can introduce you to the big ideas or purpose of the work. The foreword, generally written by someone else, serves as an extended endorsement and introduction to the work. The dedication can help one identify important influences on the author, any assistance the author has had in writing or editing the text, and even possibly a bit about the author's values or tone. Similarly, an epilogue, which comes at the end of the book, serves as a summary, final comment, conclusion, or additional information for the text. It can wrap up the book or hint at more ideas that will be developed in another work. All of these features work in conjunction with the table of contents to give the reader the big picture of the theological work.

PUTTING IT ALL TOGETHER: AN EXAMPLE OF EXAMINING THE COVER AND PUBLICATION INFORMATION

If, for example, someone is studying the book of 1 Peter and wants to gain a greater understanding of the terms *elect* and *foreknowledge* (1 Peter 1:1–2), it might be helpful to turn to a resource such as *Divine Foreknowledge: Four Views.*[5] How should one begin to examine this text with discernment? The title and publication information indicate that this work is part of a Spectrum Multiview Book Series and is considered an intermediate-level text.[6] It is published by IVP Academic, an extension of InterVarsity Christian Fellowship, an Evangelical organization that seeks to serve those in "the university, the church, and the world by publishing resources that equip and encourage people to follow Jesus as Savior and Lord in all of life."[7]

---

5. James K. Beilby and Paul R. Eddy, eds., *Divine Foreknowledge: Four Views* (Downers Grove, IL: InterVarsity, 2001).

6. "Spectrum Multiview Book Series, *Divine Foreknowledge*," www.ivpress .com/divine-foreknowledge.

7. "About IVP," InterVarsity Press, www.ivpress.com/about.

Divine Foreknowledge: Four Views was first published in 2001 and written shortly before that time. The back cover and introduction to the work mention that it was published amidst heated debates about divine foreknowledge occurring in Evangelical circles, particularly regarding the orthodoxy of open theism, the view that God does not know the future in exhaustive detail, but leaves it partially "open" to "possibilities" that are determined by a creature's free acts, as presented by Greg Boyd in this volume.[8]

The introduction also enlightens the reader to the target audience: "educated laypeople and college students who have had a first course in theology or philosophy."[9] The back cover explains that this book will help the reader identify areas of agreement and disagreement and evaluate the strengths and weaknesses of each view to help frame one's understanding of God's divine foreknowledge. All of this information is helpful in discerning not only *what* the authors are communicating, but also *why* they are delivering it in the manner they do.

The copyright and introduction also alert the reader that this work was written at the beginning of the twenty-first century. The climate in Evangelicalism in North America was very different in 2001 than it was in 1971, prior to the publication of the Chicago Statement on Biblical Inerrancy, which was written to defend biblical inerrancy from more liberal conceptions of Scripture. As the introduction of *Divine Foreknowledge* indicates, many Evangelicals, particularly in North America, saw open theism, like the inerrancy debates, as one of the next great threats to Evangelical orthodoxy.[10]

The table of contents informs the reader about not only

---

8. Gregory Boyd, "The Open-Theism View," in *Divine Foreknowledge: Four Views*, ed. James K. Beilby and Paul R. Eddy (Downers Grove, IL: InterVarsity, 2001), 13–64.

9. Beilby and Eddy, eds., *Divine Foreknowledge*, 11.

10. Beilby and Eddy, eds., *Divine Foreknowledge*, 9.

the format of the book but also the four specific views covered in this work: Gregory A. Boyd's "Open-Theism View," David Hunt's "Simple-Foreknowledge View," William Lane Craig's "Middle-Knowledge View," and Paul Helm's "Augustinian-Calvinist View." Each chapter also includes responses from the other authors.

While this book does not include endorsements, the back cover provides important introductory information about the various authors and the editors. From it, one can learn that the two editors have taught at Bethel College in St. Paul, Minnesota, which was at the time of the book's publication part of the Baptist General Conference that was discussing the orthodoxy of open theism. All of the authors write from an Evangelical perspective.

The sample above illustrates the value of starting with the publication information, introduction, and table of contents. This initial information offers insight into the book's context, content, and purpose. Through these, it is evident that this volume is primarily targeting an educated Evangelical audience with some basic philosophical and theological knowledge and is interested in the ongoing debate among Evangelicals about divine foreknowledge.

EXAMINING OTHER TEXTUAL FEATURES: WHAT DO THE NOTES, BIBLIOGRAPHY, AND INDEX TELL US?

Other textual features also help unpack a work. The often neglected footnotes/endnotes, bibliography, and index are valuable resources for answering questions such as the following, which we will examine in more depth:

- What types of sources does the author rely on?
- Who has influenced the author?
- What parts of Scripture does the author cite?

What Types of Sources Does the Author Rely On and Who Has Influenced the Author?

An author can depend on various types of sources, including science, philosophy, theology, biblical studies, Scripture, or personal experience, as well as specific theologians, philosophers, and schools of thought. It can also be important to note the sources that the author is refuting. You can begin to determine the author's sources by examining the footnotes/endnotes, internal citations, bibliography, and index. Many readers often neglect these valuable resources. A quick scan, however, can help determine what the author is primarily basing his or her ideas on. You should look not only for what types of sources the author utilizes but also for how often they cite them. For example, when you look at *She Who Is*, it is quickly evident that Elizabeth Johnson primarily relies on the experience of women, which she says is "a resource seldom considered in the history of theology."[11] She includes women who differ in race, class, culture, and other historical aspects but who share in experiences of patriarchy.

It is helpful to remember that older works, however, often lack citations. In earlier times, authors were not expected to cite their sources and often did not even have the opportunity to do so. The Bible, for instance, has not always been arranged in chapters and verses. It was not until the mid-sixteenth century that Bibles were printed with chapters and verses. Thus theologians from the past such as Martin Luther would not have noted Bible verses in the manner we do today. In these situations, it is helpful to use annotated texts, which often provide this information—such as The Annotated Luther series published by Fortress Press—or attempt to identify sources based on the content rather than on footnotes or endnotes.

---

11. Elizabeth A. Johnson, *She Who Is: The Mystery of God in Feminist Theological Discourse* (New York: Crossroad, 1992), 29.

What Parts of Scripture Does the Author Cite?

If the author relies on Scripture, it is helpful to identify which parts of Scripture the author primarily turns to, such as the Gospels, the Epistles, narrative texts, prophetic texts, wisdom literature, poetic texts, and so forth. Just as with identifying the types of sources, the reader can begin to determine the author's use of Scripture by looking at the table of contents, scanning the text, notes, and index.

Dietrich Bonhoeffer's classic work *The Cost of Discipleship*, for example, draws on the Sermon on the Mount. This leaning is not evident in the internal citations and footnotes, since Bonhoeffer does not always cite the passages, but it is revealed in the table of contents.[12]

It can be equally important to identify the parts of Scripture that the author does not use. For instance, Adolf von Harnack in *What Is Christianity?* heavily cites the Synoptic Gospels, but neglects the significance of the gospel of John, which reflects his repudiation of the full divine nature of Christ.[13] The passages that an author uses or avoids reveals much about his or her theological perspective.

PUTTING IT ALL TOGETHER: AN EXAMPLE OF EXAMINING OTHER TEXTUAL FEATURES

Quite a bit can also be gleaned by examining other textual features. Returning to our previous example, *Divine Foreknowledge: Four Views*, one can learn a lot from the notes, index, and bibliography of Greg Boyd's chapter on open theism. In his footnotes, Boyd references philosophical and scientific sources—including references to chaos theory, as well as

---

12. See Dietrich Bonhoeffer, *The Cost of Discipleship* (New York: Macmillan, 1963), 5.

13. See Adolf von Harnack, *What Is Christianity?* (New York: Putnam, 1902), 21–40.

theologians such as John Sanders and Dietrich Bonhoeffer—in support of his view. He also identifies some of his opponents, including Thomas Oden and Robert Strimple. The footnotes and Scripture index reveal Boyd's heavy reliance on Scripture. He tends to favor narrative and prophetic texts, especially from the Old Testament, over the Law and the Epistles. This approach sharply contrasts with that of two other contributors to the book, Paul Helm and David Hunt, who prioritize the New Testament Epistles. These textual features help us begin to discern some of the differences between open theism and the other perspectives in this particular book.

CONCLUSION

The importance of examining textual features and publication information is often overlooked. When this step is skipped, however, you can end up spending a lot of extra time, in the long run, trying to understand the book. It would be like trying to drive a car in reverse without first checking your mirrors. The textual features of a book serve as a guide to help you navigate the text, just as mirrors help you safely navigate your car. The author and publisher provide these tools to help you understand the text. When you use them well, you will have a good start in accurately hearing the author. As Walt Disney rightly said, "There is more treasure in books than in all the pirates' loot on Treasure Island."[14] We can begin to access that treasure by starting with this step.

---

14. Dave Smith, *The Quotable Walt Disney* (New York: Disney, 2001), 155.

QUESTIONS FOR DISCUSSION AND REFLECTION

1. Respond to the adage "Don't judge a book by its cover." Explain how judging a book *solely* by its outside appearance might be detrimental.
2. In John 7:24, Jesus says, "Do not judge by appearances, but judge with right judgment." Apply this statement to how you approach reading a book. What is one practical way you can have "right judgment" when initially examining a book?
3. What can you learn from the title of this book or from other initial textual material?
4. Publishers have different concerns and gear their works to particular audiences and areas of interest. If you were to publish a theological work, what kind of publisher would you look for, and why?
5. How might dating of a work impact your understanding of the text? Give an example.
6. Translations of texts can add an interpretative layer. Give an example of a word or phrase in English that if not adequately explained could be misunderstood. How might this same situation apply to reading theology?

PRACTICE EXAMINING TEXTUAL FEATURES AND PUBLICATION INFORMATION

What do the textual features and
publication information convey?

Briefly examine the cover, table of contents, introduction, notes, bibliography, and index of a theological book and answer the following questions:

- What is the significance of the title of the work?
- Who wrote this work?
- Who published the work?

- When was the work originally written and published?
- What edition is the work and is it a translation?
- Who is the intended audience?
- What is the purpose of the work?
- Who has endorsed the work?
- What types of sources does the author rely on? Who has influenced the author?
- What parts of Scripture does the author cite?

Briefly summarize this information and explain how it helps prepare you to read the book.

CHAPTER 4

Identifying the Context: Getting Better Acquainted with the Theologian

I have suffered a great deal from writers who have quoted this or that sentence of mine, either out of its context or in juxtaposition to some incongruous matter which quite distorted my meaning, or destroyed it altogether.

ALFRED NORTH WHITEHEAD,
DIALOGUES OF ALFRED NORTH WHITEHEAD

So we fix our eyes not on what is seen, but on what is unseen, since what is seen is temporary, but what is unseen is eternal.

2 CORINTHIANS 4:18 NIV

HOW DOES THE CONTEXT INFORM THE
MEANING OF THE THEOLOGICAL WORK?

We are, at least at one point in our lives, encouraged to take the road "less traveled." Robert Frost's famous poem "The Road Not Taken" is often quoted at graduations as a charge to make our own way in life, to resist conformity, to take risks. Ironically, Frost's well-known line "I took the one less traveled by, and that has made all the difference" has been largely misunderstood. The poet was not encouraging individuality and independence, but rather was mocking it.

Frost wrote the poem as a joke to his poet friend Edward Thomas, who was indecisive and often second-guessed his decision about which path they should have taken on their walks. At the time the poem was written, Thomas was also struggling with whether to enlist in World War I. In a letter to Thomas, Frost commented, "No matter which road you take, you'll always sigh, and wish you'd taken another." Having initially misread the poem, not recognizing it as a criticism of his indecisiveness and self-doubt, Thomas warned Frost that most readers would misunderstand it. "I doubt if you can get anybody to see the fun of the thing without showing them and advising them which kind of laugh they are to turn on."[1] After reading the poem to a group of college students, Frost reported to Thomas that it was taken too seriously, "despite doing my best to make it obvious by my manner that I was fooling . . . Mea culpa."[2]

---

1. Cited in Matthew Hollis, *Now All Roads Lead to France: A Life of Edward Thomas* (New York: Norton, 2011), 235–36.

2. Quoted in Katherine Robinson, "Robert Frost: 'The Road Not Taken,'" Poetry Foundation, May 27, 2016, www.poetryfoundation.org/articles/89511 /robert-frost-the-road-not-taken.

Without the backstory, the "sigh" in the last stanza of the poem is often enigmatic to the reader. Is it one of disappointment or of satisfaction for having taken one road over another? Is the reader to follow in the footsteps of the narrator and take the road less traveled? The way one answers these questions is somewhat dependent on the context, or on the lens through which the poem is read.

As a nineteenth-century scientist, John Lubbock, rightly said, "What we see depends mainly on what we look for." The farmer, geologist, botanist, artist, and sportsman will all notice different things in the same field: the crop, the fossils, the flowers, the colors, or the cover for hunting.[3] The same can be said about a reader. Our interpretation of a text can be influenced by the lens through which we view it.

While a poem like "The Road Not Taken" can have many interpretations, the context—or backstory—can help unpack the author's intended meaning. For Westerners who value individualism, self-determination, and freedom, the obvious meaning of the "sigh" is delight when one decides not to conform, but instead to follow one's own desires. But for Frost, a critic of the idea of self-determination, the "sigh" was intended to be, in his own words, a "mock sigh."[4] If we want to truly understand a work, we need to avoid merely reading it through our own lens, to fit our preconceptions. Instead, we should try to see the text from the author's perspective so we can hear its intended meaning.

Context plays a crucial role in determining the meaning not only of poems but also of theological texts. The context includes not only information about the *Sitz im Leben* (the situation in life or setting) of the text, but also information about the theologian's background, frame of reference, and intended

---

3. John Lubbock, *The Beauties of Nature and the Wonders of the World We Live In* (New York: Macmillan, 1897), 3.

4. Quoted in Robinson, "Robert Frost: 'The Road Not Taken.'"

audience. If we are to hear the theologian accurately, as he or she intended to be heard, we need to recognize a text's social, historical, and religious context and the intended goal of the text. We also need to recognize the presuppositions that tend to shape our interpretation of what we read.

THE SETTING

What is the context or setting?

Sitz im Leben is a German phrase that means the "situation in life," or the setting out of which a particular narrative arises. Generally, form critics have used the term to refer to the specific sociological context that gave rise to a biblical text. German scholar Hermann Gunkel, for example, used this term to signify the situation in which a particular biblical narrative was created, preserved, or transmitted.[5] While there is debate over how this concept should be applied to biblical texts—a product of divine inspiration penned by human authors (2 Timothy 3:16)—recognizing the *Sitz im Leben* is extremely helpful in unpacking theological texts, which are human works written by fallible human authors who are also influenced by their context. Therefore, we should never approach a theological work as if it were written in a vacuum.

As 1 John 4:1–6 admonishes, we are to test theological teachings. For example, in Acts 15, we are told of the controversy over whether or not Gentiles needed to be circumcised. Paul rejects imposing the Jewish practice on new converts, insisting that Gentiles do not need to become Jews to be accepted by God. For the Jews, circumcision was a major part of their identity that set them apart from the rest of the world. For the Gentiles, circumcision was an act of self-mutilation.

---

5. See F. L. Cross and E. A. Livingstone, eds., *The Oxford Dictionary of the Christian Church* (Oxford: Oxford University Press, 2005), 627.

Paul understands how the context of both the Jews and the Gentiles shapes their interpretation of circumcision. Therefore, he advocates that forcing Gentiles to be circumcised is not only meaningless but even dangerous, for it challenges the very gospel that we are saved by grace, not by works. Some of the early Jewish Christians, who were some of the earliest theologians, were imposing their own Jewish identity on the Gentiles by requiring circumcision.

When reading theology, as the above example makes evident, identifying the specific setting, or context, of a work helps the reader correctly interpret the work. This step includes determining the relevant sociopolitical situation, the ecclesiastical setting, and the goal of the theologian. Two important questions that we will consider in greater depth regarding the setting of a theological work are these:

- What is the specific context of the work?
- Why did the theologian write the work?

What Is the Specific Context of the Work?

It is essential to determine the specific social, political, and church setting surrounding the formulation of the text. This may include discovering specific situations, ideas, and events that are relevant. Just as your conversations are best understood within their particular context, so too is a theological work best understood within its particular context.

Imagine you are teaching about the pouring out of the Holy Spirit in Acts 2. What you teach will probably depend on the specific context. If you are teaching a lesson to preschoolers in a noncharismatic, cessationist (a term found in the glossary) church that maintains that the miraculous gifts spoken about in Acts were just for that time, your message is going to be different than if you are teaching a group of adults in a charismatic, continuationist setting. In the first instance, you will probably focus on who the Holy Spirit is and what the Holy Spirit did in spreading the good news of the gospel in a straightforward manner. In the second setting, you may emphasize how sign gifts—miraculous gifts of the Holy Spirit spoken of in Acts 2—are still for today. The specific audience and church will impact how and what you communicate.

The same is true for a theological text. For example, John Hick's approach to explaining a pluralist view in the book *Four Views on Salvation in a Pluralistic World* is shaped by the Evangelical audience the book was written for. The book grew out of a 1992 conference at Wheaton College on the challenges posed by pluralism and inclusivism. In the introduction, the book suggests that "Hick effectively taunts evangelicals with that haunting question: If Christians really do have more direct connection with God—the unique reality of the Holy Spirit and his fruits—should they not be morally superior to believers in other religions?"[6]

His original audience not only shapes the questions he raises, but also the way he supports his contentions with Scripture and reason. Though Hick does not believe that Scripture is the ultimate authority, it is a powerful argument with an audience that values Scripture. If he were writing to a secular audience, his approach would probably be very different.

Why Did the Theologian Write the Work?

It is essential to examine the explicit and implicit motives and goals of the theologian. In other words, to discover *who* the theologian is addressing and *what* the theologian is trying to accomplish. Is this work written in opposition to or in support of an idea? Is it written in regard to a general or specific situation? Is it written to educate, defend, or entertain?

---

6. Stanley N. Gundry, Dennis L. Okholm, and Timothy R. Phillips, eds., *Four Views on Salvation in a Pluralistic World* (Grand Rapids: Zondervan, 1996), 18.

Some theologians may clearly lay out their motives, whereas others may be much less direct.

In some cases, you may need to read between the lines to discover the theologian's purpose. For example, in the first edition of his *Institutes of the Christian Religion*, written in 1536, John Calvin writes the following in his prefatory address to the king of France:

> My purpose was solely to transmit certain rudiments by which those who are touched with any zeal for religion might be shaped to true godliness. And I understood this labor especially for our French countrymen, very many of whom I knew to be hungering and thirsting for Christ . . . The book itself witnesses that this was my intention, adapted as it is to a simple and, you may say, elementary form of teaching.[7]

At that point, Calvin intended his work to be a handbook of doctrine and a confession of faith for the novice. His purpose, however, somewhat shifted in his later editions. In his preface to the 1559 edition, he wrote to the reader, "It has been my purpose in this labor to prepare and instruct candidates in sacred theology for the reading of the divine Word, in order that they may be able both to have easy access to it and to advance in it without stumbling."[8] While he aimed the first edition toward a general Christian audience to help guide them in their understanding of the faith, he directed his revised editions more explicitly toward ministry students to train them in how to interpret and teach God's Word. This shift impacted the content and the manner in which Calvin writes.

---

7. *Inst.*, 9.
8. *Inst.*, 4.

PUTTING IT ALL TOGETHER: AN EXAMPLE OF IDENTIFYING THE CONTEXT

If, for instance, you are interested in studying the Reformed doctrine of *sola scriptura*, you may come across a short work by John Whiteford called *Sola Scriptura: An Orthodox Analysis of the Cornerstone of Reformation Theology*.[9] While the topic of *sola scriptura* is not new, with the concept predating Martin Luther in the sixteenth century, the specific context of this work is essential for understanding the theologian's position. Though the publication date of the pamphlet is 1997, a bit of research reveals that it was actually written a few years earlier, when Whiteford was a Reader at St. Vladimir Orthodox Church in Houston, shortly after he had converted from the Nazarene faith. It is important to recognize, as he mentions at the beginning of the text, that the mid-1990s saw the dissolution of the Soviet Union, whose pre-Soviet religious identity was primarily Russian Orthodox, and an influx of Protestant missionaries into Russia.

This work was first published in 1995 in *The Christian Activist*, a journal of the Russian Orthodox Church, and reissued in 1996 as a monograph of Conciliar Press, a publishing house of the Orthodox Church in America. Whiteford made it clear that his primary intended audience was lifelong members of the Orthodox Church, to help them understand the critical presuppositional and epistemological differences between Protestant and Orthodox systems of faith. By pointing out the fallacies of Protestantism, he sought to prevent Orthodox members from leaving the Orthodox Church. He also intended to appeal to disillusioned Protestants who might want to explore the Orthodox faith.

When this work is read with this specific context in mind, one becomes aware of Whiteford's agenda—to protect Orthodox

---

9. John Whiteford, *Sola Scriptura: An Orthodox Analysis of the Cornerstone of Reformation Theology* (Ben Lomand, CA: Conciliar, 1997).

members from being led astray by Protestants. Writing primarily to an Orthodox audience, he assumes that they understand and value the Orthodox tradition and maintain that the Orthodox Church is the one true church. He also assumes they do not know a lot about Protestantism and writes in broad generalizations, comparing Protestantism to a mythical, poisonous, multiheaded Hydra, lumping Mormons and Jehovah's Witnesses together with Protestants. Whiteford is more intent on supporting the Orthodox Church in this work than on giving an unbiased explanation of *sola scriptura*. Knowing the author's context and goals brings his *Sola Scriptura* into sharp contrast with *The Shape of Sola Scriptura*, written by Reformed Christian theologian Keith Mathison in 2001.[10]

BACKGROUND: GETTING MORE ACQUAINTED WITH THE THEOLOGIAN

Who is the author?

A second step in discovering crucial contextual information is becoming more acquainted with the theologian. The author's background, frame of reference, role, and presuppositions inform *what* and *how* he or she writes. Just as the botanist and artist make different observations about the same field, so too the philosophical and practical theologian or the Eastern Orthodox and Reformed Christian make different observations about the same biblical texts.

Often, reliable biographical information can be found in the book itself. Publishers typically provide valuable information about the theologian on the book cover or in the foreword, preface, or introduction. Further information can also be discovered on publishers' websites and in reputable academic resources, such

---

10. Keith A. Mathison, *The Shape of Sola Scriptura* (Moscow, ID: Canon, 2001).

as the websites for the university, the church, or the ministry that the author works for. It is generally best to avoid popular websites such as Wikipedia, where it is difficult to determine the reliability of the information provided. Instead, credible resources written by experts on the person or topic and published by reputable publishers or web domains are preferable. If using online sources, it is helpful to find information published by university websites (.edu) or professional organizations (.org).

If you cannot find enough information from the publisher or theologian, as is often the case with older theological works, university libraries often provide access to credible online resources, such as specialized encyclopedias and databases. Even when information is found on a reputable academic site, one still needs to be aware that biases can exist. For instance, if you're trying to find out the background of Martin Luther's *Bondage of the Will*, Mormon scholar A. Burt Horsley from Brigham Young University will give you a very different picture of the Reformer than leading Luther scholar Martin Brecht.

Some of the background questions that should be addressed are the following:

- What is the theologian's specific background and frame of reference?
- What are the theologian's presuppositions?

What Is the Theologian's Specific Background and Frame of Reference?

The theologian's background includes his or her religious/denominational background, educational training, ethnic background, and sociopolitical background. Just as our taste buds impact our experiences of the foods we eat, so too do our backgrounds impact our theological perspectives. Though we are not merely a product of our environment, our experiences and education have a shaping influence on our lives. Rarely, if ever, do we make decisions that are not informed in some way by our background, whether that be advice we've received or experiences we've had. Our parents, teachers, church, race, social circumstances, and gender can all have a formative impact on our theological perspectives. We should keep this in mind when we are reading theology.

Theologians are influenced by where they grew up, whom they studied under, and what situations they have faced. Their backgrounds inform their worldviews. Theologians can speak from a number of positions—as a feminist, a liberation theologian, a revisionist, a pragmatist, an Evangelical, an Arminian, a Calvinist, a Roman Catholic, a Lutheran, or an Eastern Orthodox. Their frame of reference will further be addressed in chapter 5 on discerning theological frameworks.

What Are the Theologian's Presuppositions?

A presupposition is an implicit supposition or control belief that shapes an author's perspective. In other words, it is an assumption that something is true, whether or not it has been verified. We all hold presuppositions that impact our perspective of God and the world. For instance, most Americans presuppose that freedom is a natural, inalienable right. Other countries, cultures, and time periods do not share this presupposition. This presupposition affects how Americans view justice, human rights, and even our relationship with God.

The answers to the following questions help one identify a theologian's presuppositions:

- What is authoritative?
- What is reality?
- Who is God?
- Who are we and where did we come from?
- What is the problem that needs to be resolved?
- What is the remedy?

It is helpful to listen for the subtle nuances in a theologian's answer to these questions. Particularly with regard what is authoritative, their answer will impact all their other propositions. For example, both Martin Luther and Ulrich Zwingli insisted that Scripture is the supreme and final authority in matters of faith. These Reformers stressed the importance of the authority of Scripture over and against the Roman Catholic Church's insistence on the authoritative nature of the church and its tradition.

Luther and Zwingli differed, however, in their presupposition about the value of human reason. Zwingli, trained as a Christian humanist, valued reason far more than Luther did. This disparity is evident in their debate at Marburg over the nature of the Lord's Supper. Luther contended that the bread and the wine were in some way the body and blood of Christ because Christ says, "This is my body." According to Luther, we are to take God at his word. In contrast, Zwingli, valuing reason, argued that the "is" in the words of Christ should be understood as "signifies," just as the "I am" sayings of Christ in the gospel of John are to be read metaphorically. Christ is not literally a door or a vine; so too he is not literally in the bread and the wine. While both theologians held to the authority of Scripture above all else, Zwingli held that revelation and reason could not contradict, whereas Luther maintained that revelation often contradicts human reason. Their presuppositions had a significant impact on their theology about the sacraments and Christ.

PUTTING IT ALL TOGETHER: AN EXAMPLE OF IDENTIFYING BACKGROUND AND PRESUPPOSITIONS

Much can be learned about Denis O. Lamoureux, one of the authors of the book *Four Views on the Historical Adam*, from the opening pages of the book and back cover. Lamoureux has a PhD in Evangelical theology from the University of St. Michael's College, as well as a PhD in evolutionary biology and a DDS from the University of Alberta. At the time of the publication, he was an associate professor of science and religion at St. Joseph's College, a Catholic liberal arts college on the campus of the University of Alberta. His position is "the first tenure-track position in Canada dedicated to teaching and research on the relationship between scientific discovery and Christian faith."[11]

He has authored a number of books, including *Evolutionary Creation: A Christian Approach to Evolution*; *I Love Jesus and I Accept Evolution*; and *Darwinism Defeated? The Johnson-Lamoureux Debate on Biological Origins*. These works help us discover that Lamoureux has exegetically and scientifically sought to defend evolution from an Evangelical perspective.

St. Joseph's website points out that Lamoureux's academic focus is on the modern origins controversy, embracing "the time-honored belief that there are two major sources of Divine revelation—the Book of God's Words and the Book of God's Works. The Bible and the physical world complement each other." He holds that science discloses *How* God created the world, whereas the Holy Scripture attests to *Who* created it. Without both Divine Books, we have incomplete knowledge. He maintains that the "Father, Son, and Holy Spirit created the universe and life through an ordained, sustained, and design-reflecting evolutionary process." The Bible should not be seen as a science book, but rather as offering "inerrant, life-changing, Messages of Faith."[12]

In his personal story, Lamoureux shares how he was raised

---

11. Stanley N. Gundry, Matthew Barrett, and Ardel B. Canedy, eds., *Four Views on the Historical Adam* (Grand Rapids: Zondervan, 2013), 7.

12. "Denis O. Lamoureux DDS, PhD, PhD," St. Joseph's College, https://sites.ualberta.ca/~dlamoure.

as a Roman Catholic and lost his childhood faith as a university student after studying evolutionary biology. The scientific worldview that he was surrounded by—with the core assumption that truth must be scientifically validated—led him to see religion as "only an illusion and an accidental by-product of human evolution." When he returned to his faith many years later, he initially rejected evolution for young earth creationism and biblical literalism as held by many conservative Evangelicals. He then went on to complete two PhDs, one in theology and one in biology, to help make sense of the question of origins. It was during that time that he became an evolutionary creationist, an unpopular position in Evangelical circles. He maintains that this position makes sense of the Two Divine Books—creation and the Bible.[13]

This information gives a lot of valuable insights into his presuppositions and motives for arguing for an evolutionary creation view of the historical Adam. For Lamoureux, this is not merely an abstract theological discussion, but one that helps answer the critical question of origins. This is a question that has been a stumbling block for many people, including Lamoureux himself.

From the book and St. Joseph's website, we learn essential information about his educational background and expertise, pointing to how he stands apart from the other contributors of the book with his evolutionary creation view. His personal narrative gives insights into his presuppositions, including his beliefs that there are two Divine Books—the Bible and creation—that God is personal and works through orderly processes such as evolution; that we are sinful beings created to be in a relationship with God; and that we are in need of redemption by Christ.

---

13. Denis O. Lamoureux, "Coming to Terms with Evolution: A Personal Story," https://sites.ualberta.ca/~dlamoure/3_personal_story_ec.pdf.

The first of these presuppositions makes a crucial difference in his perspective. Though he identifies himself as a conservative Evangelical scholar, being a member of the Evangelical Theological Society, he is also a scientist. He, unlike the other contributors, maintains that the Bible has an ancient understanding of nature that can and should be challenged by the book of science.

To unpack the meaning of this information, it is helpful to look at resources such as Walter Elwell's *Evangelical Dictionary of Theology* and H. Wayne House's *Charts of Christian Theology and Doctrine*.[14] Both of these sources will help readers of theology begin to understand the background information that they discover, such as what is evolution, evolutionary creationism, young earth creationism, the historical Adam, and biblical literalism. With an understanding of these terms, one can be equipped to more fully understand Lamoureux's perspective on the historical Adam.

CONCLUSION

The more one knows about a theologian and the context of a work, the more one is equipped to be a good dialogue partner. Just as one has a deeper understanding of what is being communicated by a friend or family member than by a stranger, so is it with a theological text that one has taken time to get to know. You are less likely to give the same weight to the opinion of a stranger than a trusted friend regarding the value of a movie or a novel. Why should it be any different for a theological text? When the theologian you are reading stays a stranger, it is difficult to know whether you should accept his

---

14. Daniel J. Treier and Walter A. Elwell, eds., *Evangelical Dictionary of Theology*, 3rd ed. (Grand Rapids: Baker Academic, 2017); H. Wayne House, *Charts of Christian Theology and Doctrine* (Grand Rapids: Zondervan, 1992).

or her perspective, much less have confidence that you even understand what he or she is trying to say.

We can misread a theological text if we skip this step, just like many have misinterpreted Frost's poem "The Road Not Taken." Frost's friend Thomas Edward was well aware of the potential for this poem to be misunderstood. Edward, who was a close friend, had initially misread it. It was only after a number of communications with Frost that he was able to understand the true meaning of Frost's composition. Knowing the poet and his motives helped him grasp the true meaning.

Philosopher Alfred North Whitehead makes a similar point when he discusses the problem of thinking of taking words out of their context. He writes, "I have suffered a great deal from writers who have quoted this or that sentence of mine, either out of its context or in juxtaposition to some incongruous matter which quite distorted my meaning, or destroyed it altogether."[15] Both the words and ideas of a theologian must be understood within their context.

The answers to contextual questions help tell us the backstory of a theological work. The questioning, however, should not end there. We should also ask these questions of ourselves. By doing so, we can begin to identify the lens from which we may naturally view the theological works we read, as well as the world we live in. Are we, like Frost, skeptical of our ability to determine our future by the simple everyday decisions we make? Do we see *sola scriptura*, like Whiteford, as a heresy? Do we, like Lamoureux, look to science to help answer the questions of our origin?

How we answer these questions depends in large part on our backstory. Our context impacts not only how we evaluate other people's opinions, but also how we form our views

---

15. Alfred North Whitehead, *Dialogues of Alfred North Whitehead* (1956; repr., Boston: Godine, 2001), 225.

and live our lives. We may not always be conscious of the lens through which we view the world, but it is still there. As Alfred Whitehead rightly said, "A philosopher of imposing stature doesn't think in a vacuum. Even his most abstract ideas are, to some extent, conditioned by what is or is not known in the time when he lives."[16] How much more could this be said of us? We are influenced by our culture, faith, personality, upbringing, experiences, and education. The sooner we become aware of the influences, the sooner we can begin to choose what we want to allow to inform our lives. Reading theology well can help us grow more aware and hopefully correct some the unfounded biases that we may have.

QUESTIONS FOR DISCUSSION AND REFLECTION

1. The famous process philosopher Alfred North Whitehead wrote, "I have suffered a great deal from writers who have quoted this or that sentence of mine either out of its context or in juxtaposition to some incongruous matter which quite distorted my meaning, or destroyed it altogether." Give an example from your own life of either misunderstanding someone else or being misunderstood by something being taken out of its context.

2. Second Corinthians 4:18 (NIV) states, "So we fix our eyes not on what is seen, but on what is unseen, since what is seen is temporary, but what is unseen is eternal." This passage encourages us to avoid fixing our minds on our temporary afflictions and trials and instead contemplate our future glory in heaven. What are the "seen" things that shape your current worldview (or lens on reality)? What "unseen" things should shape your worldview? Practically, how can your current worldview impact how you listen and respond to theological texts? To God?

---

16. Whitehead, *Dialogues of Alfred North Whitehead*, 225.

3. Read Robert Frost's famous poem "The Road Not Taken."

> Two roads diverged in a yellow wood,
> And sorry I could not travel both
> And be one traveler, long I stood
> And looked down one as far as I could
> To where it bent in the undergrowth;
>
> Then took the other, as just as fair,
> And having perhaps the better claim,
> Because it was grassy and wanted wear;
> Though as for that the passing there
> Had worn them really about the same,
>
> And both that morning equally lay
> In leaves no step had trodden black.
> Oh, I kept the first for another day!
> Yet knowing how way leads on to way,
> I doubted if I should ever come back.
>
> I shall be telling this with a sigh
> Somewhere ages and ages hence:
> Two roads diverged in a wood, and I—
> I took the one less traveled by,
> And that has made all the difference.[17]

What current Western cultural values inform how this poem is commonly understood?

What difference does it make in your understanding of the poem to know the backstory—that it was written as a joke, mocking his friend Edward Thomas's indecisiveness and regret after choosing one of two possible paths?

---

17. Robert Frost, "The Road Not Taken," www.poetryfoundation.org/poems/44272/the-road-not-taken.

4. Identify your presuppositions by answering the following questions:
   - What is authoritative?
   - What is reality?
   - Who is God?
   - Who are we and where did we come from?
   - What is wrong?
   - What is the remedy?
5. How do these answers inform the way you respond to the following questions?
   - What is your role in determining your future?
   - How authoritative is Scripture? The church?
   - What is the role of science in helping answer the questions about our origin?

PRACTICE IDENTIFYING THE CONTEXT

How does the context inform the
meaning of the theological work?

1. Pick another contributor from the book *Four Views on the Historical Adam* or a theological text you are currently reading and answer the following questions:
   - **What is the specific context of the work?** What is the specific social, political, and church setting?
   - **Why did the theologian write the work?** What are the explicit and implicit motives and goals of the theologian?
   - **What is the theologian's background?** What is the theologian's religious/denominational background, educational training, ethnic background, sociopolitical background?
   - **What is the theologian's role?** Is it the role of a narrator, a pastor, a scientist, a philosopher, a teacher, a spiritual mentor, an apologist, or a historian?
   - **What are the theologian's presuppositions? What are the theologian's views about?**

- What is authoritative?
- What is reality?
- Who is God?
- Who we are and where did we come from?
- What is wrong?
- What is the remedy?

2. How does the above information help you discern the meaning of the theological text?

Discerning Theological Frameworks: Identifying the Theme of the Work and How It Is Conveyed

If a book is easy and fits nicely into all your language conventions and thought forms, then you probably will not grow much from reading it. It may be entertaining, but not enlarging to your understanding. It's the hard books that count. Raking is easy, but all you get is leaves; digging is hard, but you might find diamonds.

MORTIMER J. ADLER, *HOW TO READ A BOOK*

And he gave the apostles, the prophets, the evangelists, the shepherds and teachers, to equip the saints for the work of ministry, for building up the body of Christ, until we all attain to the unity of the faith and of the knowledge of the Son of God . . . so that we may no longer be children, tossed to and fro by the waves . . . Rather, speaking the truth in love, we are to grow up in every way into him who is the head, into Christ, from whom the whole body, joined and held together by every joint with which it is equipped, when each part is working properly, makes the body grow so that it builds itself up in love.

EPHESIANS 4:11–16

71

What makes good art? When it adheres to certain design principles? When it is beautiful? When it accurately portrays something? When it impacts your worldview? When it elicits an emotional response? Say, for instance, you are asked your opinion about Pablo Picasso's famous painting *Girl before a Mirror*. How do you evaluate it? With its intense colors, thick black lines, and busy backdrop, this two-dimensional painting of Marie-Thérèse Walter gazing into a mirror is not initially considered beautiful by most people.

For you to truly appreciate Picasso's masterpiece, it is helpful to understand his artistic approach. While he was trained as a Realist, Picasso developed Cubism to challenge the notion that art is merely an act of imitation rather than one of creativity. With Cubism, he abandoned an objective perspective for a highly symbolic, challenging, and multifaceted one. Picasso's cubist depiction of Marie-Thérèse Walter is radically different, as it should be, from his realistic drawings and sculptures of her. This work demands an emotional response. When gazing at this painting, the well-trained viewer has the opportunity to wrestle with themes such as beauty, fertility, aging, self-image, and vanity.

In the same way Picasso uses the medium of paint and the Cubist style in *Girl before a Mirror* to communicate a message, a theologian employs a type of work and an approach to express his or her theological views. Just as an artist can paint, draw, or sculpt, a theologian can write a polemic, a systematic work, or a sermon on a variety of themes. Just as a painter can employ Realism, Impressionism, or Cubism, a theologian can use a historical, rational, or experiential approach. Knowing the topic and the framework of a theological work can help unpack the presuppositions, goals, and meaning of the text. To ascertain these, the reader should seek to discover the following:

- What is the topic?
- What type of theologian is the author?
- What type of theological work is it?
- What theological approach does the theologian utilize?

The first question deals with *what* the work is about, and the latter questions with *how* it is communicated.

ADDRESSING THE *WHAT* QUESTION:
What is the topic of the work?

Theologians cover a variety of topics, often even in the same work. Traditionally, the major topics of theology are as follows:

- **Method of Theology (Prolegomena):** This area includes all introductory matters of theology. It consists of the nature and task of theology, issues of how you do theology (methodology), how we acquire knowledge (epistemology), and what the sources of theology are.
- **Revelation:** This doctrine includes how God reveals God's nature, will, and truth. It consists of the nature and purpose of general and special revelation, the preservation of revelation, and the dependability of God's Word.
- **God (Theology Proper):** Theology proper is the study of God. It includes the existence and knowledge of God, the nature of God, the work of God, and the Trinity.
- **Christ (Christology):** The doctrine of Christ includes the nature and work of Jesus Christ.
- **Holy Spirit (Pneumatology):** The doctrine of the Holy Spirit includes the person and work of the Holy Spirit.
- **Creation:** The doctrine of creation includes the creation of the world and the cosmos, God's relation to creation, the state of the original creation, the Sabbath, the impact of the fall on creation, angels, and creation care.

- **Humanity (Anthropology):** The doctrine of humanity is often viewed as a subtopic of the doctrine of creation. It includes the origin of humankind, the image of God in humanity, gender, the constitutional nature of humans, and the purpose of life.
- **The Fall/Sin (Hamartiology):** The doctrine of the fall and sin is often seen as a subtopic of anthropology. It includes the doctrine of evil, an understanding of the fall, the consequences of the fall, the nature of sin, the source of sin, humanity's relationship with Adam, the results of sin, and the individual and social dimensions of sin.
- **Salvation (Soteriology):** The doctrine of salvation includes God's planning of salvation, God's providing redemption in history, God's applying salvation to the individual, and God's completion of salvation.
- **The Church (Ecclesiology):** The doctrine of the church includes the nature of the church, the purpose of the church, the power of the church, the role and government of the church, the ordinances (sacraments) of the church (including baptism and the Lord's Supper), and worship in the church.
- **The Christian Life:** The doctrine of the Christian life includes the topics of discipleship, obedience, holiness, sanctification, perseverance, and Christian virtues and ethics.
- **The Future (Eschatology):** The doctrine of the future includes death, the second coming of Christ, views on the millennium and tribulation, the final judgment and eternal punishment, and the new heaven and the new earth.

The choice of topics and the order in which they are discussed can impact the conclusions the theologian makes. For example, under what general topic does a theologian discuss the foreknowledge of God? Does the theologian explain it under the doctrine of creation, as Greg Boyd does, or under the doctrine of God, as John Piper does?[1] If the theologian sets it under the doctrine of creation or anthropology, then generally the focus will be on its compatibility with human freedom. If the theologian places it under the doctrine of God, the focus will be on God's sovereign character.

It is also essential to read between the lines when examining the topic of a theological work. It can be just as important to be aware of what is *not* covered as of what *is* included. For example, when one examines Adolf von Harnack's treatment of Christ in *What Is Christianity?* it is essential to observe that a discussion of Christ's divinity is conspicuously missing. There could be a number of reasons why the author focuses on the humanity and not the divinity of Christ. It may be that he addresses the deity of Christ in another writing, that he is dealing with a particular passage that focuses on Christ's humanity, that he sees a need for the audience to recognize the full humanity of Christ, or that he doesn't believe in Christ's divinity. Noticing the absence of an expected topic can be a vital piece of information.

ADDRESSING THE *HOW* QUESTION

What method does the theologian use to approach the subject matter?

Theologians use a number of methods to communicate their theology. To more fully understand *what* they are communicating, it is essential to understand *how* they are communicating. One only needs to think about the impact that literary techniques such as sarcasm can have on the meaning of a text to begin to recognize the significance that the mode of communication can have on understanding a theological work. How

---

1. Beilby and Eddy, eds., *Divine Foreknowledge: Four Views*, 13–14; John Piper, *Beyond the Bounds: Open Theism and the Undermining of Biblical Christianity* (Wheaton, IL: Crossway, 2003).

are you to understand, for example, Exodus 14:11, which reads, "Is it because there are no graves in Egypt that you have taken us away to die in the wilderness? What have you done to us in bringing us out of Egypt?" Are the Israelites actually wondering if Moses brought them out of Egypt because there was no place to bury them, or are they murmuring against him? Theological genres, like literary techniques such as sarcasm, can significantly impact the communication of theological knowledge.

The ability to identify theological approaches increases as one becomes more conscious of the lens or orientation of the theologian and *how* the theologian presents his or her ideas. Awareness can begin before one even starts reading a text simply by looking at information given by the publisher, theologian, or outside sources. Sometimes theologians will explicitly state their theological orientation; other times they will communicate it implicitly.

Identifying the theological genres can help the reader gain a deeper knowledge of a theologian's convictions. This step, however, can be one of the most challenging tasks of reading theology well, in part because most readers are not very familiar with the different types of theology, much less the various theological approaches that an author may employ. In addition, many theologians do not necessarily adhere to one framework. In ascertaining the theologian's approach, the reader should seek to discern three things: the type of theologian, the type of work, and the theological approach, which includes the structure, framework, and sources. The last of these will be covered in the next chapter.

What Type of Theologian Is the Author?

Most theologians specialize in a particular type of theology and write from a specific perspective. An author can write from the position of a narrator, a pastor, a scientist, a philosopher, a teacher, a spiritual mentor, an apologist, a historian, or a person who has a particular racial, social, or gender perspective. Of course, you will find some theologians who fit into multiple categories, such as Jonathan Edwards, who wrote as a pastor, a theologian, a philosopher, a scientist, an ethicist, a poet, and a devotional writer. It is helpful, however, to understand some of the broad categories that theologians can fall under. Here are just a handful:

Biblical theologian. Seeks to discover what the biblical writers, such as John or Paul, under divine guidance, believed, described, and taught in the context of their historical setting. This is primarily a descriptive type of theology.
- *Examples:* Geerhardus Vos, D. A. Carson, N. T. Wright

Systematic theologian. Attempts to express in unified constructs the biblical teaching on theological topics such as the doctrine of Christ, anthropology, or the Trinity.
- *Examples:* John Calvin, Karl Barth, Millard Erickson

Historical theologian. Investigates the development of Christian thought through church history.
- *Examples:* Jaroslav Pelikan, Louis Berkhof, Alister McGrath

Practical theologian. Focuses on the practical application of biblical truths in modern life.
- *Examples:* Richard Baxter, Charles Spurgeon, Ray S. Anderson

Moral theologian/Christian ethicist. Examines the relationship between the Bible and real-life situations, problems, and needs, including topics such as medical and sexual ethics.
- *Examples:* Augustine, Stanley Hauerwas, Oliver O'Donovan

Philosophical theologian. Uses philosophical reflection, language, and methods with the aim of gaining a theoretical understanding of the nature and character of God and God's relationship with the world.
- *Examples:* Thomas Aquinas, Paul Tillich, Alvin Plantinga

Ideological theologian. Explores the relationship between Christian theology and particular ideologies and views theology from a specific perspective, often that of the oppressed. This approach usually emphasizes the need for upholding social justice and human rights and seeing Jesus as Savior and Liberator. This category includes liberation, black, and feminist theologians.

- *Examples:* Gustavo Gutiérrez, James Cone, Dorothee Sölle

Apologist. Defends the Christian faith through systematic, argumentative, or pragmatic discourse.

- *Examples:* Justin Martyr, C. S. Lewis, William Lane Craig

What Type of Theological Work Is It?

There are not only many types of theologians, but also many genres of theological works. Just as you can classify a book as fiction or nonfiction, practical or theoretical, academic or popular, adult or children's, most theological works can be classified. An author can articulate their theology using some of the following genres:

Sermon/Lecture. An oration expounding on biblical passages or theological topics.

- *Example:* Martin Luther King Jr., *Death of Evil upon the Seashore*

Theological treatise/Essay. An exposition or argument treating a theological topic in depth and investigating the principles of the topic.

- *Example:* Jonathan Edwards, *A Treatise Concerning Religious Affections*

Polemic. A theological argument addressing an important, controversial topic, often written as an attack or a defense of a belief.

- *Example:* Martin Luther, *The Babylonian Captivity*

Dialectic/Response. A theological analysis including a dialogue with or reaction to a specific idea or theological work. It may be written in a question/answer or dialogue format. Medieval Scholastics and neoorthodox theologians often used this genre.

- *Example:* Anselm, *Why God Became Man*

Creed/Confession. A formal declaration of principle articles of faith of a church or religious group.

- *Example:* Apostles' Creed

Catechism. Summary of the principles of faith in the form of questions and answers that are used for the instruction of Christians.

- *Example:* Heidelberg Catechism

Commentary. A systematic series of explanations of the background and meaning of biblical passages, typically organized by book, chapter, and verse.

- *Example:* Karl Barth, *Epistle to the Romans*

Theological reference work. Reference works include theological dictionaries, encyclopedias, and study Bibles. The entries or reference notes are often theological in nature.

- *Examples:* David Wright, Sinclair Ferguson, and J. I. Packer, eds., *New Dictionary of Theology*; Scofield Study Bible (Includes dispensational interpretations of Scripture)

Systematic work. A systematic study of what the Bible teaches on various topics in Scripture.

- *Example:* John Calvin, *Institutes of the Christian Religion*

Satire. A work that holds up vices and follies in order to expose, ridicule, or discredit them.

- *Example:* Erasmus, *In Praise of Folly*

Story/Novel/Allegory/Play. Literature written to illustrate biblical truths or Christian experiences.

- *Example:* John Bunyan, *The Pilgrim's Progress*

Poetry. The use of figurative language to convey biblical truths or Christian experiences.
  - *Example:* John Milton, *Paradise Lost* and *Paradise Regained*

Hymn/Prayer. A song or prayer written to worship God.
  - *Example:* Thomas Ken, *Doxology*

Autobiography/Biography/Memoir. An inspiring story of the life of a Christian.
  - *Example:* Augustine, *Confessions*

Apologetic work. A theological work written in defense of the Christian faith.
  - *Example:* Justin Martyr, *First Apology*

Mystical work. A description of an experiential knowledge of God, often including ecstatic visions of God and descriptions of the soul's union with God.
  - *Example:* Julian of Norwich, *Revelations of Divine Love*

Devotional work. Christian literature written for spiritual formation.
  - *Example:* A. W. Tozer, *The Pursuit of God*

While some theologians, such as Julian of Norwich, stick to one type of work, many employ various genres, depending on *what* they are communicating, *why* they are communicating it, and *who* their audience is. For instance, Dorothy Sayers wrote novels, essays, poems, plays, and books that were theological in nature. While her twelve-part play *The Man Born to Be a King* about the life of Jesus was broadcast on the radio by the BBC to a secular audience, her theological treatise *The Mind of the Maker* is directed to a Christian audience. Recognizing the type of work can greatly aid in interpreting a work. Another example is Erasmus's *In Praise of Folly*, which can be easily misinterpreted if one does not recognize it as a satire and reads it as a literal theological treatise.

What Theological Approach Does the Theologian Utilize?

Not only can a theologian employ a particular type of theology, literary genre, or topic, but he or she can also utilize a specific theological approach. Just as artists can employ different styles, such as Realism, Impressionism, or Cubism, theologians can use different theological frameworks to convey their ideas. In the area of biblical interpretation, there are many approaches, ranging from very literal to very metaphorical or even practical.[2] Theologians, like biblical scholars, also approach theology in a particular manner. It is essential to understand *how* a theologian approaches theology. There are whole books devoted to explaining theological methods. These books attempt to categorize methodologies by their starting points, foundational basis, ideology, or the formal structure of their works.[3] All of these approaches have some merit.

---

2. Some of the biblical interpretative approaches are Literal, Allegorical, Source, Tradition-Historical, Form, Redaction, Social-Scientific, Canonical, Rhetorical, Structural, Narrative, Reader-Response, Post-structuralist, and Feminist. Understanding methods of biblical interpretation can be overwhelming, even for theologians. This list is by no means intended to be exhaustive or sufficient for explaining all the interpretative approaches. Further descriptions and examples of the various methodological approaches of biblical interpretation can be found in William W. Klein, Craig Blomberg, Robert L. Hubbard, and Kermit Allen Ecklebarger, *Introduction to Biblical Interpretation*, 3rd ed. (Dallas, TX: Word, 2017); Stephen R. Haynes and Steven L. McKenzie, *To Each Its Own Meaning*, rev. ed. (Louisville, KY: Westminster John Knox, 1999); and Stanley E. Porter and Beth M. Stovell, eds., *Biblical Hermeneutics: Five Views* (Downers Grove, IL: IVP Academic, 2012). Historical criticism can be further broken down into various methodologies such as: canonical criticism, form criticism, redaction criticism, source criticism, tradition criticism, and so forth (Richard N. Soulen, *Handbook of Biblical Criticism* [Atlanta: Knox, 1981], 79). For the purpose of introducing oneself to methodologies, however, I advocate using a simplified list that helps you begin to recognize the use of different interpretative approaches and how they help you understand the author's perspective.

3. There are many helpful resources to help you understand theological approaches. Bernard Lonergan's *Method in Theology* (Toronto: University of Toronto Press, 1971) is helpful in grasping the incredible range of theological methods. A more brief, practical survey of how theologians historically have spoken about God is available in Paul L. Allen's *Theological Method: A Guide for*

It should be noted, however, that theological works rarely follow strict methods, like scientific inquiry or even methods of biblical interpretation. This is particularly true of historical works, where methodological concerns tend to be more implicit rather than explicit. In the past century, however, with the rise of the modern scientific approach, theologians have been much more attentive to and explicit about their theological method. It is now commonplace for theologians to acknowledge the basis of their views, their aim, and even the manner in which they communicate their theology. The focus here is to give a broad overview of *how* various theologians can pursue truth, recognizing that these categories are not comprehensive and cannot account for every theologian. Below are some of the possible approaches:

Propositional/Rationalist propositional approach. The pursuit of truth by uncovering the intended meaning of the text. The task is to gather biblical data and formulate theological principles from the information.[4] Scripture is generally regarded as the foundation for theology, which can be accessed and interpreted by reason. Conservative Evangelicalism and Fundamentalism are often associated with this approach.

    o *Example:* Carl Henry, *God, Revelation, and Authority*

Experiential/Experimental approach. The pursuit of truth by direct interaction of the soul with God or by natural religious consciousness. Religious feelings, intuition, or rational experiences of the individual are seen as the

---

the Perplexed (London: T&T Clark, 2012). One that can aid you understanding current ideological methodologies is Mary M. Veeneman's *Introducing Theological Method: A Survey of Contemporary Theologians and Approaches* (Grand Rapids: Baker Academic, 2017). An important work on the relationship between philosophy and theology is Diogenes Allen's *Philosophy for Understanding Theology* (Louisville, KY: Westminster John Knox, 1985).

    4. See Stanley Porter and Steven M. Studebaker, eds., *Evangelical Theological Method: Five Views* (Downers Grove, IL: IVP Academic, 2018), 8.

normative source of truth rather than the Bible alone. This approach assumes that truth can be discovered in the realm of human experience. Protestant liberalism and mysticism could be placed under this approach.

- ○ *Example:* Friedrich Schleiermacher, *The Christian Faith*

Systematic approach. The pursuit of truth through faith and human reason. It aims at developing a logically coherent and rationally defensible system of what the Bible teaches on a given topic. Medieval Scholasticism and Protestant Scholasticism could be placed under this approach.

- ○ *Example:* Francis Turretin, *Institutes of Elenctic Theology*

Historical approach. The pursuit of truth by understanding the world behind the biblical text. It assumes that historical analysis is necessary for understanding the past and uncovering the actual message of Scripture. Some liberal theologians could be placed under this approach.

- ○ *Example:* Adolf von Harnack, *History of Dogma*

Praxis approach.[5] The pursuit of truth by seeing the current reality as foundational. Interpretation begins and ends with the current social reality. This approach is often committed to the struggle for justice, and practical concerns shape the reading and interpreting of Scripture. Liberation, feminist, black, *mujerista*, and womanist theology could fall under this orientation.

- ○ *Example:* Elizabeth A. Johnson, *She Who Is: The Mystery of God in Feminist Theological Discourse*

Neoorthodox approach. The pursuit of truth by encountering God in the Word. In contrast to propositionalism (which prioritizes the Bible) and experientialism (which prioritizes reason/experience), this approach emphasizes the revelation of God himself as the foundation of Christian

---

5. Daniel Migliore uses this term to explain this approach in *Faith Seeking Understanding: An Introduction to Christian Theology* (Grand Rapids: Eerdmans, 2014), 17.

beliefs. The Bible is regarded as an instrument that is a witness to the true Word of God, Jesus Christ. This approach often seeks to find truth in opposites and paradoxes.

  o *Example:* Karl Barth, *Church Dogmatics*

Postliberalism/Narrative approach. The pursuit of truth by utilizing a cultural-linguistic approach to theology. Doctrines are seen as shaping and providing the structure for individual religious experience. It emphasizes the authority of the person of Christ and the biblical narratives over the historic truthfulness or inerrancy of Scripture. The focus is primarily on the beliefs and practices of the Christian community.

  o *Example:* George Lindbeck, *The Nature of Doctrine*

Postconservative approach. The pursuit of truth by moving beyond a propositional theology while still centering theology on the Bible. This approach often defers to tradition and orthodox doctrine critically and constructively.

  o *Example:* Stanley Grenz, *Theology for the Community of God*

Correlational approach. The pursuit of truth by discovering the correlation between Christian revelation and the contemporary understanding of human existence. Revelation must speak to and make sense of the current situation. Revisionist theology, which seeks to reformulate truth claims according to correlation of Christian texts and human experience, would fall under this category.

  o *Example:* Paul Tillich, *Systematic Theology*

The categories above are intended to provide a very general overview of how theologians may pursue knowledge of God and creation's relationship to God. At best, however, these categories should be seen as approaches, attitudes, or orientations rather than as strict methodologies. One should be aware that discussions on theological method often focus on the questions of the "what" and "why" of theology rather than on the practical question of "how" to do theology.

PUTTING IT ALL TOGETHER: AN EXAMPLE OF DISCERNING THEOLOGICAL FRAMEWORKS

The work of the eighteenth-century American theologian Jonathan Edwards offers a compelling example of the importance of understanding an author's theological framework. Depending on which of his works you read, you could wind up with a widely divergent understanding of his theology. For example, Edwards's *Freedom of the Will* or *Sinners in the Hands of an Angry God* would create a very different impression on a reader than his *Personal Narrative*. While each of these works covers similar themes regarding human nature, depravity, and God's will and sovereign grace, Edwards employs different theological genres to critique libertarianism, to promote revival, and to share his personal understanding of grace. One work is a theological treatise, one a sermon, and one an autobiographical spiritual work. One text primarily employs a rational and philosophical approach, one a propositional and narrative approach, and one a more experiential approach.

Each of Edwards's texts serves the same overarching aim of communicating truths about human depravity and God's sovereignty and grace, but each is tailored to a different audience and context. *Freedom of the Will* was written to an academic audience to refute Arminianism. *Sinners in the Hands of an Angry God* was written during the Great Awakening to promote revival. Edwards penned his *Personal Narrative* to fellow Christians to recount his conversion and to encourage them in their faith. If his use of different theological genres is ignored, one could misread Edwards as strictly a deterministic philosopher, a hellfire preacher, or a religious mystic.

CONCLUSION

Discerning theological frameworks is essential to fully grasping a theologian's perspective. Reading works that cover complex themes and are written in an unfamiliar style or approach requires effort and perseverance. As Mortimer Adler rightly points out, however, "If a book is easy and fits nicely into all your language conventions and thought forms, then you probably will not grow much from reading it. It may be entertaining, but not enlarging to your understanding." He insists that "it's the hard books that count. Raking is easy, but all you get is leaves; digging is hard, but you might find diamonds."[6]

We need to be willing to do the hard work of digging into complex theological works if we want to find the diamonds of God's truth. Just as understanding Picasso's Cubist approach enables us to understand and appreciate *A Girl before a Mirror*, familiarizing ourselves with a theologian's framework will help us understand his or her work and discover the diamonds within it. Awareness begins before one even begins reading by looking at information given by the publisher, author, or even outside sources. It continues by reading the text and the footnotes/endnotes. Identifying the theological framework, whether explicit or implicit, will help the reader gain a more profound knowledge of a theologian's convictions.

QUESTIONS FOR DISCUSSION AND REFLECTION

1. Pablo Picasso depicts Marie-Thérèse Walter in many works of art. Compare *Girl before a Mirror* with one of his sketches of her. How do the Cubist and Realist approaches impact the way he depicts her? The message communicated? How might the manner in which a theologian expresses his or her ideas affect the message? Give an example.

6. Mortimer J. Adler and Charles Van Doren, *How to Read a Book: The Classic Guide to Intelligent Reading*, rev. ed. (New York: Simon & Schuster, 1972), 339.

2. Theologians can communicate about a variety of topics, even in the same work. If you were asked to teach a four-week middle school–age Sunday school class about the essentials of the faith, what topics would you include? What order would you discuss them in? How do the topics and the order impact your aims?

3. Jonathan Edwards has primarily been depicted as a fiery Puritan who preached the famous sermon *Sinners in the Hands of an Angry God* during the Great Awakening. He also served as one of the first presidents of Princeton University and was well known even during his lifetime for his philosophical and theological treatises. How would you classify Edwards as a theologian, and why? How does the classification impact our view of Edwards's theology?

4. Theologians can articulate their theology in many different ways. Erasmus, a classically trained Christian humanist, utilizes satire in his work *In Praise of Folly* to criticize and poke fun at the traditions and abuses of the Roman Catholic Church. Written to his friend Sir Thomas More, this work is considered one of the most important works of the Renaissance, which made a significant contribution to the beginnings of the Protestant Reformation. Do you think satire is an appropriate genre for theologians to utilize today? What are the pros and cons of using this type of literature? What type of genre is most appropriate in academic circles today? In churches? In popular culture?

5. How to pursue truth is a fundamental question that theologians grapple with. What difference does it make if a theologian approaches writing about the Christian life from a propositional or an experiential approach? How could it practically impact his or her view of gender identity, for example?

6. In Ephesians 4:11–16, Paul describes many different callings in equipping the saints for ministry. We are all theologians called to know God and share that knowledge with others. As a theologian, what do you see as your calling? How would you respond if someone asked you to describe what type of theologian you are and how you attempt to pursue truth?

7. Mortimer Adler insists, "If a book is easy and fits nicely into all your language conventions and thought forms, then you probably will not grow much from reading it. It may be entertaining, but not enlarging to your understanding. It's the hard books that count. Raking is easy, but all you get is leaves; digging is hard, but you might find diamonds." Give an example of a theological work that was challenging to understand, but one you benefited from reading.

PRACTICE DISCERNING THEOLOGICAL FRAMEWORKS

What *is the theme of the theological work and how is it conveyed?*

1. Briefly examine a theological work and answer the following questions:
   Addressing the What Question:
   - What is the topic of it?

   Addressing the How Question:
   - What type of theologian is the author?
   - What type of theological work is it?
   - What theological approach does the theologian use?
2. Briefly summarize in a few sentences *what* the theme of the work is and *how* it is conveyed.
3. How does this information help you better understand the aim, message, and value of the work?

CHAPTER 6

Discovering the Sources: Identifying the Foundations of the Work

A person who is a good and true Christian should realize that truth belongs to his Lord, wherever it is found, gathering and acknowledging it even in pagan literature, but rejecting superstitious vanities.

AUGUSTINE OF HIPPO, *ON CHRISTIAN DOCTRINE*

For although they knew God, they did not honor him as God or give thanks to him, but they became futile in their thinking, and their foolish hearts were darkened. Claiming to be wise, they became fools, and exchanged the glory of the immortal God for images resembling mortal man and birds and animals and creeping things.

ROMANS 1:21–23

What are the theologian's foundational sources?

"I feel, therefore I am." This could be considered the current mantra of science and popular thought rather than René Descartes's "I think, therefore I am." Emotions seem to have displaced philosophical reasoning as the determiner of truth. Books such as *Descartes' Error: Emotion, Reason, and the Human Brain* by neurophysiologist Antonio Damasio are drawing new attention to the critical role that emotions play in cognition and identity.[1]

Damasio argues that all human identity is a kind of fiction and that we are all in the process of self-creation, claiming that "there is the very simple self, the core self, something for which you do not need memory, for which you do not need language—you just have a feeling of being."[2] What is the source of our identity? Of truth? Is Damasio correct that there is no true source of human identity, only a "feeling of being"? What can we learn from neuroscience? From sources other than Scripture? Theologians have wrestled with this last question in particular throughout history. More recently, many, like Damasio, have turned to feelings as a primary source of truth.

The sources that theologians utilize can impact their theology. It is essential not only to identify *what* sources theologians use but also *how* they employ them. Do they prioritize specific sources? Are their sources foundational to or being used in support of their theological views? Asking these types of questions

---

1. Antonio Damasio, *Descartes' Error: Emotion, Reason, and the Human Brain* (New York: HarperCollins, 1994); for an overview, see Emily Eakin, "I Feel, There I Am," *New York Times*, April 19, 2003, www.nytimes.com/2003/04/19 /books/i-feel-therefore-i-am.html.

2. Quoted in Tim Radford, "I Feel, Therefore I Am," *The Guardian*, January 20, 2000, www.theguardian.com/books/2000/jan/20/scienceandnature .booksonhealth.

can give us a window into the questions of what is authoritative for the theologian and what is the aim of the work.

In 1964, Albert Outler discerned that John Wesley used four different sources in his theology: Scripture, tradition, reason, and experience. He dubbed this combination "the Wesleyan quadrilateral."[3] Outler argued that Scripture was the centerpiece of Wesley's theology, with tradition, reason, and Christian experience as dynamic and interactive aids that he used in interpreting the Word of God in Scripture.[4]

Theologians, however, have not always valued all four of these sources for theology. For instance, the early church theologian Tertullian questioned the use of reason and philosophical thinking, famously asking, "What has Athens to do with Jerusalem?" This view is in sharp contrast to René Descartes's later statement that helped build the foundation for rationalism: "I think, therefore I am."

The use of tradition as a source for theology has also been controversial. While the Roman Catholic Church pronounced the indispensable value of Tradition (that is, the Roman Catholic "sacred Tradition") at the Council of Trent, Reformers such as Martin Luther argued for *sola scriptura* (Scripture alone) as the source of theology.

Similarly, you can observe diverse views on the value of religious experience as a basis for theology. While liberal theologians such as Friedrich Schleiermacher have appealed to religious experience, claiming that the truest understanding

---

3. Outler cautions using the term without recognizing that it is not meant to mean an equal-sided figure. He wrote instead that "it was intended as a metaphor for a four element syndrome, including the four-fold guidelines of authority in Wesley's theological method. In such a quaternity, Holy Scripture is clearly unique. But this in turn is illuminated by the collective Christian wisdom of other ages and cultures between the Apostolic Age and our own" (Albert C. Outler, "The Wesleyan Quadrilateral in Wesley," *Wesleyan Theological Journal* 20, no. 1 [Spring 1985]), http://wesley.nnu.edu/fileadmin/imported_site/wesleyjournal/1985-wtj-20-1.pdf, 11.

4. See Outler, "Wesleyan Quadrilateral," 9.

of God is a "feeling of absolute dependence,"[5] respondents such as J. Gresham Machen have argued against this idea: "It is no wonder, then, that liberalism is totally different from Christianity, for the foundation is different. Christianity is founded upon the Bible. It bases upon the Bible both its thinking and its life. Liberalism, on the other hand, is founded upon the shifting emotions of sinful men."[6] Other theologians have used the natural sciences, social sciences, or other disciplines such as philosophy in their theology. Let's take a brief look at some of these possible sources.

WHAT IS THE ROLE OF SCRIPTURE?

Historically, theologians have seen Scripture as vital to theology. They have differed, however, in their view of its role and level of authority. For some, like Ulrich Zwingli, the Bible is the supernatural Word of God and the only source of truth (*sola scriptura*).[7] For other theologians, such as Karl Barth, the Bible is a "witness of divine revelation."[8] Still others, like Bart Ehrman, see it as a literary work, much like Shakespeare's plays, that communicates moral ideas that can shape and guide people today.[9]

---

5. See Friedrich Schleiermacher, *Christian Faith: A New Translation and Critical Edition*, vol. 1, ed. Catherine L. Kelsey and Terrence Tice (Louisville, KY: Westminster John Knox, 2016), 18–44.

6. J. Gresham Machen, *Christianity and Liberalism* (Grand Rapids: Eerdmans, 1923), 79.

7. "Therefore those who hear are God's sheep, are the church of God, and cannot err; for they follow the word only of God, which can in no wise deceive. But if they follow another word, they are not Christ's sheep, nor flock, nor church; for they follow a stranger. For it is characteristic of the sheep not even to hear a stranger" (Ulrich Zwingli, *Commentary on True and False Religion*, ed. Samuel Macauley Jackson and Clarence Nevin Heller [Eugene, OR: Wipf & Stock, 2015], 373).

8. Karl Barth, *The Doctrine of the Word of God*, vol. 1 of *Church Dogmatics*, ed. G. W. Bromiley and T. F. Torrance (Edinburgh: T&T Clark, 1956), 457.

9. "People need to use their intelligence to evaluate what they find to be true

Scripture's content, authority, inspiration, inerrancy, infallibility, reliability, unity, and diversity have all been areas of contention among theologians. The following questions can help unpack how a theologian views and utilizes Scripture:

- What comprises Scripture? Are the books of the Apocrypha included?
- Is Scripture the sole foundation (*sola scriptura*), the primary foundation (*prima scriptura*), or one of many foundations?
- Is Scripture a divine or human work? Is it inspired by God or is it made up of merely human accounts?
- Is Scripture inerrant (the content is without error when correctly interpreted) and infallible (trustworthy in its message)? If so, to what extent? Is it correct only in matters of faith and practice or also in historical and scientific details?
- Is Scripture propositional, narrative, metaphorical, or practical in nature? Is it descriptive, prescriptive, or corrective?
- Do certain parts of Scripture have priority over other parts of Scripture?
- How should Scripture be interpreted? Literally, figuratively, spiritually, contextually, morally?
- How contextualized is Scripture? How does the original biblical context impact the meaning of the passage?
- How applicable is Scripture today?

---

and untrue in the Bible. This is how we need to live life generally. Everything we hear and see we need to evaluate—whether the inspiring writings of the Bible or the inspiring writings of Shakespeare, Dostoevsky, or George Eliot, or Gandhi, Desmond Tutu, or the Dalai Lama . . . Then why study the Bible? . . . The Bible is the most important book in the history of Western civilization. It is the most widely purchased, the most thoroughly studied, the most highly revered, and the most completely misunderstood book—ever! Why wouldn't I want to study it?" (Bart D. Ehrman, *Jesus, Interrupted: Revealing the Hidden Contradictions in the Bible (and Why We Don't Know About Them)* [New York: HarperOne, 2009], 281–82).

How a theologian answers these questions impacts his or her use of Scripture. These are also important questions to ask ourselves. How do we view Scripture? What role does Scripture play in the development of our theology? Do we use Scripture as a foundation for our beliefs or merely as a proof text of them?

WHAT IS THE ROLE OF TRADITION AND THE CHURCH?

Another resource that has been heavily valued both implicitly and explicitly by theologians is tradition, or the teachings of the church. The word *tradition* derives from the Latin word *traditio*, meaning "to hand over or deliver." Broadly, the theological term refers to the beliefs and practices of the Christian faith that have been handed down and received by the Christian community. The nuances of the term, however, have been understood in a variety of ways.

For some, tradition refers to the passing down of the apostolic teachings and practices that are not contained in Scripture. In this sense, tradition can also refer to the authoritative teachings and interpretations of the church fathers or the popes. This could include the teachings of historic councils, creeds, confessions, and catechisms. Others maintain that tradition is the living influence of the Holy Spirit on the church. The term *church* here is often used in reference to the Roman Catholic Church or Eastern Orthodox Church, not the universal church (the whole body of Christians). In this view, the church is seen as the primary transmitter of tradition. Another perspective sees tradition as centered on church practices such as worship, prayer, and the Lord's Supper or baptism.

Generally, the Roman Catholic, Eastern Orthodox, Oriental Orthodox, and Anglican Churches have placed more emphasis on tradition than Protestants, affirming "Scripture and tradition" as foundational, interconnected sources of theology.

More recently the Roman Catholic Church has differentiated between *apostolic tradition* (the message of Christ from the Holy Spirit that has been passed down by the apostles to their successors) and *ecclesiastical tradition* (particular customs and teachings that originate within a specific church context). While both are considered authoritative, the former is seen as part of the unchangeable deposit of faith, whereas the latter can be modified or changed.[10]

Even when theologians do not explicitly use tradition as a source, they often implicitly do. For example, how theologians approach baptism is often connected with their own church practices, not just Scripture. So while a Baptist maintains that baptism is the practice of the full immersion of a believer and is a prerequisite to membership, a Lutheran holds that baptism is a miraculous means of grace and that when an infant is baptized by the sprinkling of water, God can create faith in the child's heart. Both use some of the same biblical passages as a basis for their position but rely in part on their tradition to explain their position.[11]

Some of the questions that can help unpack how a theologian understands and uses tradition are as follows:

- What is tradition comprised of? Creeds, confessions, official church statements, liturgy, worship practices?
- What is the source of tradition? Individual humans, the church, the Holy Spirit?
- What are the means for determining what is true tradition?

---

10. See "Catechism of the Catholic Church: The Transmission of Divine Revelation," www.vatican.va/archive/ccc_css/archive/catechism /p1s1c2a2.htm.

11. You can see the different expressions in the Southern Baptist Theological Seminary's 1858 statement, "Baptists on Believer's Baptism," www.baptiststart. com/print/baptism_quotes.html, and the Lutheran Church Missouri Synod's statement, "Frequently Asked Questions—Doctrine: Baptism," www.lcms.org /about/beliefs/faqs/doctrine#baptism.

- When can tradition be changed?
- How authoritative is tradition?
- What is the relationship between tradition and Scripture? Reason? Experience? Culture?

While Protestants have historically "protested" against the use of tradition as a primary source of theology, nonetheless it has had an important role in the Protestant faith, though sometimes unintentional. What role does tradition play in your own theology, whether it is following official tradition or just beliefs and practices you have consciously or unconsciously integrated from your Christian community?

WHAT IS THE ROLE OF REASON?

The word *reason* has been understood in a number of different ways. It can refer to human cognition or discernment. When used this way, it is seen as the process of using cognition in evaluating beliefs. It can also be understood as a source of knowledge. This view makes a distinction between the "truths of faith" and the "truths of reason." The former is derived from divine revelation, and the latter from natural human faculties. A third way refers to reason as logic or intellect. This perspective sees reason as an aspect of the image of God that uniquely endows humans with an intellectual nature or capacity that enables them to understand and love God and the world God created.[12]

While reason, with all of its nuances, has played a vital role in the development of theology, it has not always been recognized as a reliable source. In fact, logical, rational, and

---

12. Keith Mathison explores the topic of faith and reason and the various historic understandings ("Faith and Reason," Ligonier Ministries, www.ligonier. org/learn/articles/faith-and-reason-article); see also R. C. Sproul and Keith Mathison, *Not a Chance: God, Science, and the Revolt against Reason* (Grand Rapids: Baker, 2014).

analytic thoughts or natural human capacities have sometimes been viewed as being in direct conflict with the Christian faith.

With the rise of Scholasticism, theologians began to utilize and even rely heavily on reason, following Anselm's motto *fides quaerens intellectum*, or "faith seeking understanding." Martin Luther, however, fiercely rejected the natural capacity to reason as a basis for faith: "Reason is the greatest enemy that faith has: it never comes to the aid of spiritual things, but—more frequently than not—struggles against the Divine Word, treating with contempt all that emanates from God."[13] Luther even reportedly called reason (though one must look at the context of his statement) "the Devil's greatest whore."[14]

Other Reformers, such as John Calvin and Ulrich Zwingli, also appealed to the necessity of the gift of faith and agreed with Luther that reason on its own cannot grasp the gospel. They, however, did not share Luther's great distaste for reason. Instead, they recognized it as a valuable source with limitations in its fallen state.[15]

Below are some helpful questions to discern a theologian's perspective on reason:

- What is the nature of reason?
- What is the relationship between reason and knowledge? Truth? Faith?

---

13. Martin Luther, *The Table Talk of Martin Luther*, ed. William Hazlitt (London: Bell, 1902), 164. Luther is recorded making this statement regarding the Anabaptist refusal to baptize children based on their lack of rational capacities.

14. See Martin Luther, *Luther's Works*, vol. 51, ed. John W. Doberstein (Philadelphia: Fortress, 1973), 371–80. It should be noted that Luther in his last sermon in Wittenberg was not totally rejecting reason. Rather, he was insisting that it be "subject and obedient to this faith" (p. 379).

15. Calvin, for example, recognizes the limitations of reason: "[The gospel] is a doctrine not of the tongue but of life. It is not apprehended by the understanding and memory only, but it is received only when it possesses the whole soul, and finds a seat and resting place in the inmost affection of the heart" (*Inst.*, III.6.4).

- Is reason impacted by the fall and sin?
- Is reason universal?
- What are the strengths and weaknesses of reason?

One of the keys to understanding a theologian is addressing his or her perspective on reason—not only whether it is a valid source, but also the nature and use of it. These questions are important for the reader as well. Examining your perspective on whether reason is a natural capacity, how reliable of a source it is, and its relation to faith and truth is vital.

Underlying presuppositions about reason, especially in Western culture, often tend to strongly emphasize science and rationality, thus influencing our theological perspectives. One example is the use of reason to identify right from wrong. Thinkers such as Aristotle, Alexander Hamilton, and C. S. Lewis have all argued, based on reason, that humans have a higher calling than following base instincts. Similarly, readers often use reason to evaluate the worth of a theologian's statements and develop their own beliefs based on what seems reasonable to them.

WHAT IS THE ROLE OF EXPERIENCE?

Experience has also played a significant role in the development of theology. In general, the word *experience* means "knowledge gained by repeated trials or attempts." In theology, experience is often understood as that which relates to the inner spiritual life or perceptions of the individual. For instance, John Wesley refers to experience when he talks about his heart being "strangely warmed," and Jonathan Edwards when he describes the Christian's "new spiritual sense" or the "sense of the heart." Julian of Norwich writes about her "experience" of Christ on her deathbed when she received fifteen visions, or "shewings," directly from God. In theology, religious experiences can be seen as natural sensory perceptions, supernatural spiritual experiences, or subjective feelings.

Evangelicals, liberals, and mystics have all appealed to experience as a foundational basis for their theology. The first often appeals to the authoritative nature of personal religious experiences in conjunction with Scripture. Such is the case with John Wesley. The second often bases their theology primarily on natural perceptions and feelings. Friedrich Schleiermacher's appeal to the "feeling of absolute dependence" as the essence of religion is an example of this. The last group views supernatural, mystical revelations as not only possible but normative. Julian of Norwich saw her revelations as direct visions from God that were later confirmed as authentic by the Catholic Church.

Some of the questions that help unpack a theologian's view of and reliance on experience are the following:

- What role does experience play in conveying and determining truth?
- In what ways can one experience God and perceive truth? By feelings, visions, sensory perceptions?
- What is the source of true experience? Natural or supernatural, or a combination of these?
- How are experiences authenticated? By the church, the individual, or science?

In an age where experiences are often seen as normative, people are appealing more and more to them as an appropriate basis for theology. It is not uncommon to hear Christians defend their theological positions based on their feelings or personal experiences. No one can disagree with another person about whether or not he or she has had an experience or perceives something in a particular way. But how much weight should we give to our experiences or perceptions? Can perceptions be wrong? How do you interpret the meaning of your experiences?

These are essential questions to ask not only of the theologians we read but also of ourselves.

WHAT IS THE ROLE OF SCIENCE?

What is the relationship between science and theology? Are they friends or foes? Many conservative Christians have assumed the latter, suggesting that the acceptance of science as a viable source of theological truth is a recent and negative development. But as senior professor of Christian philosophy Nancey Murphy rightly argues, modern Western science finds its origins within "the matrix of a Christian worldview."[16] Though you can see moments of conflict between science and Christianity, for example, in the Catholic Church's treatment of Galileo Galilei in the seventeenth century, historically the Catholic Church has been one of the biggest supporters of science. In fact, historically the monasteries were centers for intellectual learning and made significant contributions to the field of science. The Catholic Church has been credited with founding many of the world's most renowned hospitals.

Genuine conflict, however, became prominent in the early twentieth century with the rise of Fundamentalism and its response to higher criticism and evolutionism. Fundamentalists saw Scripture, not science, as the authoritative source of truth. Science, therefore, must align itself with Scripture and not the other way around. The Fundamentalist approach, however, is not the only approach to science, even among conservative Christian theologians.

---

16. Nancey Murphy, "Science and Theology: Mapping the Relationship," Fuller Studio, https://fullerstudio.fuller.edu/science-theology-mapping -relationship. James Hannam discusses how Christianity helped launch science in *The Genesis of Science: How the Christian Middle Ages Launched the Scientific Revolution* (Washington, DC: Regnery, 2011).

Below are some of the questions that help unpack a theologian's view of science as a source of theology:

- How compatible are science and the Christian faith?
- How do we reconcile differences between scientific and biblical accounts of the universe?
- How reliable is science in revealing truth?
- What can science reveal about the purpose of the universe? The creation of the universe? God? Humans?
- How are we to view the "laws of nature"?
- What is the relationship between the natural and the supernatural?

WHAT IS THE ROLE OF SOCIAL CONDITIONS?

Everyone lives within a specific historical, social, political, familial, ecclesiastical, and cultural setting. While God and the truths of the gospel transcend the bounds of time, space, and social conditions, the Old and New Testaments were written at specific times, in particular places, under certain circumstances, and to specific audiences. Likewise, the interpreters of Scripture read Scripture from a particular context. Even nationality, gender, ethnicity, and language can be shaping factors in theological reflection.

Neither the writing nor the reading of Scripture happens within a vacuum. A theologian's thinking and even our interpretation of his or her ideas are significantly influenced by social conditions. For example, if theologians come from a context of oppression, they tend to address very different questions than if they come from a context of privilege. This contrast is evident when one compares the works of Gustavo Gutiérrez with Joel Osteen. Both writers address issues of wealth and liberation, but from radically different perspectives.

Gutiérrez, a Peruvian theologian, encourages his readers

to adopt a Marxist reading of the Gospels that focuses on caring for the needs of the poor.[17] In contrast, multimillionaire American megachurch pastor Osteen encourages his listeners to see God's generosity toward his committed disciples. Rather than encouraging his audience to give to the poor, he advises them to increase their "capacity to receive."[18] Social settings can have a tremendous influence on the lens through which a theologian views Scripture and the concerns that he or she brings to the text.

Some helpful questions to identify how social conditions can serve as a source of theology are as follows:

- What is the theologian's specific social context from which he or she is writing?
- How do they understand their social situation?
- How does their social context influence or shape their theology?
- How do they address their context or another context in their theology?

These questions are also productive questions for the reader of theology to ask of oneself. For instance, do the American values of liberty and justice for all influence our response to the theological perspectives on divine foreknowledge? If we came from a more hierarchical culture, would we have the same perspective? Rarely, if ever, are we able to suspend the influence of our social conditions and make unbiased theological judgments.

---

17. Gustavo Gutiérrez, *A Theology of Liberation* (Maryknoll, NY: Orbis, 1973). Gutierrez wrote, "The praxis on which liberation theology reflects is a praxis of solidarity in the interests of liberation and is inspired by the gospel" (p. xxx).

18. Joel Osteen, *Break Out! 5 Keys to Go beyond Your Barriers and Live an Extraordinary Life* (New York: FaithWords, 2013), 47.

WHAT ABOUT THE ROLE OF OTHER DISCIPLINES?

What is the relationship between theology and other disciplines such as literary criticism, archaeology, sociology, psychology, and philosophy? Some theologians have sought to isolate Christian theology from the findings of other disciplines, while others have abandoned long-held theological beliefs in favor of the "new knowledge" discovered by other fields.[19] Still others have sought to integrate theology and other disciplines, adhering to the principle "all truth is God's truth." Augustine holds this position: "Let every good and true Christian understand that wherever truth may be found, it belongs to his Master."[20] Interestingly, John Calvin, a proponent of *sola scriptura* (Scripture alone), also shares this perspective. In his *Institutes*, he even insists that one can learn by "reading profane [secular] authors" in whom "the admirable light of truth is displayed" even in their fallen condition. We need to be careful, according to Calvin, that we "neither reject the truth itself, nor despise it wherever it shall appear."[21]

Many theologians maintain that God speaks by both natural and supernatural revelation. The question remains, however, of what to do when the "new knowledge" discovered by natural revelation appears to contradict Scripture. For example, it has been "discovered" by Israeli archaeologists that camels were not domesticated in Israel until the ninth century BC.[22] Yet the biblical accounts portray camels being domesticated from the time of Moses. Which account is correct? Does this discovery

---

19. Douglas F. Ottati addresses this in "Christian Theology and Other Disciplines," *Journal of Religion* 64, no. 2 (April 1984): 173–87.

20. Augustine, *On Christian Doctrine*, trans. J. F. Shaw (Mineola, NY: Dover, 2009), 53.

21. *Inst.*, II.2.15.

22. Morgan Lee, "New Evidence Using Carbon Dating Contradicts the Bible, Israeli Archeologists Claim," *Christian Post*, February 6, 2014, www .christianpost.com/news/new-evidence-carbon-dating-contradicts-bible-israeli -archeologists-claim-114116.

mean that the Bible is not historically reliable? Theologians vary widely in their views of the value of other disciplines and how much weight they should be given.

Some critical questions to be asked about the use of other disciplines are as follows:

- Where does God reveal truth? Which disciplines contain truth?
- How valid are the findings of other disciplines?
- What is the relationship of theology to other disciplines? Which has primary authority?
- How do you reconcile contradictions between Scripture and other disciplines?
- When is it appropriate to integrate other disciplines and when should they be kept separate?

PUTTING IT ALL TOGETHER: AN EXAMPLE OF IDENTIFYING THE SOURCE

The significant role that sources can play in a theologian's perspective is evident in the recent monism-dualism debate on human composition. Historically, Christian theologians have favored a dualistic understanding of human nature—that is to say, humans are comprised of two substances: physical and spiritual. While some theologians, particularly in the East, have argued that the nonphysical aspect of humans can be further divided into a soul and spirit, generally theologians have still been aligned on a dualistic perspective of humanity, or "substance dualism."

Recently, however, the dualistic view of human composition has come under fire, particularly by scholars invested in other academic disciplines. Christian theologian and philosopher of science Nancey Murphy is one such scholar. Murphy addresses the critical issue of the nature of human beings in her book *Bodies and Souls, or Spirited Bodies?* In this work, she defends a

"nonreductive physicalist" account of human nature, asserting
that "we are our bodies—there is no additional metaphysical
element such as mind or soul or spirit."[23] On what basis does
Murphy conclude that humans are comprised of only one part,
or what she calls "Spirited bodies?"

Murphy's theology of human composition is informed by
critical biblical scholarship, current scientific theory, and contemporary philosophy. Murphy uses critical biblical scholarship
to argue that a physicalist account of human nature does not
conflict with a biblical view because "the Bible has no clear
teaching here."[24] She argues that past scholars have errantly
read a dualistic position into the text based on imprecise translations and dualistic presuppositions.

Murphy also explains why advances in scientific understanding undermine a dualist orientation, appealing to the
Copernican Revolution and the Darwinian theory of evolution. She argues that the evidence from physics, evolutionary
biology, and neuroscience better support a physicalist position.[25]
Based on current philosophical thought, Murphy contends that
the monistic view still allows for free will and human responsibility. She also includes vague allusions to personal spiritual
encounters, including her divine call to theological education.

This work was written as part of a series on "Current Issues
in Theology" for nonacademics, so Murphy attempts to give
a basic survey of the history of religious, scientific, and philosophical views of human nature rather than a biblical account.
Relying heavily on other disciplines, Murphy reveals her
presupposition that natural reason is a valid and foundational
source for understanding human nature. She suggests that
humans can have encounters with the divine and that Scripture

---

23. Nancey Murphy, *Bodies and Souls, or Spirited Bodies?* (New York :
Cambridge University Press, 2006), ix.

24. Murphy, *Bodies and Souls, or Spirited Bodies?* 4.

25. See Murphy, *Bodies and Souls, or Spirited Bodies?* 48–49, 56.

is a valuable Christian source but not the primary basis of her theological position. For Murphy, Christianity and science are compatible, and God primarily works by natural means.

CONCLUSION

Truth—where can it be found? In Scripture? Tradition? The church? Reason? Experience? Science? Society? Which sources do we prioritize? Every theologian must answer these questions. While Augustine of Hippo sees Scripture as the primary source of truth, he still maintains, like Nancey Murphy, that God can reveal truth through natural means as well:

> A person who is a good and a true Christian should realize that truth belongs to his Lord, wherever it is found, gathering and acknowledging it even in pagan literature, but rejecting superstitious vanities and deploring and avoiding those who "though they knew God did not glorify him as God or give thanks but became enfeebled in their own thoughts and plunged their senseless minds into darkness. Claiming to be wise they became fools, and exchanged the glory of the incorruptible God for the image of corruptible mortals and animals and reptiles."[26]

He bases his understanding of the validity of natural revelation on Romans 1:21–23, encouraging his audience to recognize truth in the world. He, however, also acknowledges the need to separate the wheat from the chaff. We are not to blindly accept all sources as equally valid. He reminds his readers that due to the fall, many have exchanged God's truths for senseless lies. We, too, need to consider how we distinguish valid sources of truth from "superstitious vanities."

---

26. Saint Augustine, *On Christian Teaching* (Oxford: Oxford University Press, 1997), 47.

QUESTIONS FOR DISCUSSION AND REFLECTION

1. What sources are used in the seeking of truth today in society? Give a specific example.

2. The Wesleyan quadrilateral is a method of theological reflection credited to John Wesley that identifies the use of four sources to reach theological conclusions: Scripture, tradition, reason, and experience—with Scripture being the centerpiece. How have you seen sources prioritized in current theological reflection? What has been the place of Scripture?

3. Though there have been many perspectives on the value of tradition, it has had a significant role in shaping theological reflection. Come up with some examples of how tradition has shaped theology. How have you seen it as instrumental in Protestant theology?

4. The use of science and other disciplines in theological reflection has been debated among theologians. Some have sought to integrate faith and science, for example, while others have seen them at odds with one another. What do you see as the relationship between natural means of knowledge and theological reflection? Is science a foundational source of truth about God and God's relationship with the world? If so, what do we do when science and Scripture seem to contradict one another?

5. Social settings can have a tremendous influence on the lens through which a theologian views Scripture and the concerns he or she brings to the text. How does your setting impact the way you read the Bible? Theology?

6. Respond to Augustine's statement—"Let every good and true Christian understand that wherever truth may be found, it belongs to his Master." Where do you think truth can be found? How do we discern God's truth from what Augustine calls "superstitious vanities"?

PRACTICE IDENTIFYING THE SOURCES

What sources does the theologian utilize?

Briefly examine a theological work and answer the following questions:

1. What types of sources does the theologian utilize? Be specific. Scripture, tradition, the church, reason, experience, science, social conditions, other?
2. How does the theologian utilize the sources?
   - Does the theologian prioritize specific sources?
   - Are the sources foundational to or being used in support of their theological views?
3. What does this information tell you about the question of what is authoritative for the theologian and what the aim of the work is?

CHAPTER 7

Discerning the Theologian's View: Listening for the Main Contention, Key Points, and Key Terms

I consider as lovers of books, not those who keep their books hidden in their store-chests and never handle them, but those who, by nightly as well as daily use, thumb them, batter them, wear them out, who fill out all the margins with annotations of many kinds, and who prefer the marks of a fault they have erased to a neat copy full of faults.

ERASMUS, *CORRESPONDENCE,*
VOL. 1 IN *COLLECTED WORKS OF ERASMUS*

The hearing ear and the seeing eye,
the LORD has made them both.
PROVERBS 20:12

What is the theologian seeking to communicate?

Are you a good listener? Eugene Raudsepp tells the story of a zoologist who while walking down a busy city street exclaims to his friend, "Listen to that cricket!" The friend responds with astonishment, saying, "You hear a cricket in the middle of all this noise and confusion?" The zoologist carefully reaches into his pocket, takes out a coin, flips it into the air, and allows it to fall to the ground. A dozen people turn their heads in response to the clink of the coin on the concrete. Then the zoologist quietly responds to his friend, "We hear what we listen for."[1] Isn't that often true in conversations? Even the words of our beloved friends can be muffled by the noise and confusion of our minds.

The heart of dialoguing with anyone lies in being able to actively listen and grasp what is really important to that person. Unfortunately, most of us are not as good at listening as we should be. While virtually everyone deems themselves an effective communicator, research has shown that the average person only listens with a 25 percent rate of efficiency.[2] Truly effective communicators, however, are experts in listening. Novelist Ernest Hemingway pointed out the value of attentive listening: "I like to listen. I have learned a great deal from listening carefully. Most people never listen."[3] Being an effective listener and communicator is a biblical concept. James 1:19 calls the believer to be "quick to hear, slow to speak, slow to anger."

---

1. Eugene Raudsepp, "The Art of Listening Well," *Inc.*, October 1, 1981, www.inc.com/magazine/19811001/33.html.

2. Cited in Lindsay Holmes, "9 Things Good Listeners Do Differently," *HuffPost*, August 14, 2014, www.huffpost.com/entry/habits-of-good-listeners_n_5668590; see the study by Richard Huseman, James M. Lahiff, and John M. Penrose on communication (*Business Communication: Strategies and Skills* [Chicago: Dryden, 1991]).

3. Quoted in "Active Listening: Small Group Activity," BYU Center for Teaching and Learning," https://ctl.byu.edu/tip/active-listening-small-group-activity.

Good communication—namely, communication that involves actively listening and being open to considering another person's perspective, is a basic element of true friendship and wisdom. Reading theology well, like active listening, is an art that requires work, skill, and attentiveness. To be a good conversation partner with a theological text, one must be able to understand and consider the theologian's viewpoint. As Mortimer Adler wrote, "Enlightenment is achieved, only when, in addition to knowing what the author says, you know what he means and why he says it."[4]

This dialogue becomes possible once the reader can do three things: identify the aim of the work, ascertain the main arguments, and apprehend the critical terms of the text. The listening process begins by asking the right questions of the work.

The following questions are helpful in enabling one to listen well to a theological text:

- **What is the theologian contending in the work?** What is the thesis, and what are the key points?
- **What are the key terms that are important in understanding the theologian's perspective?** Identify and define both the words in the text you don't know and the words that are important to the theologian's arguments.

With these questions in mind, one should begin reading with a pencil, stylus, or keyboard in hand. Active reading, like active listening, requires engagement. It involves attending, understanding, interpreting, recalling, reflecting, clarifying, and summarizing what the author communicates in the text. Just as in listening, however, there are many barriers that can interfere. Some are external, such as environmental distractions

---

4. Mortimer J. Adler and Charles Van Doren, *How to Read a Book* (New York: Simon & Schuster, 1972), 11.

like loud noises. More often, however, the distractions are internal. These can include personal biases, lack of interest, or lack of context to be able to understand a text. Marking up the text or taking notes can help overcome those distractions and enable the reader to engage more deeply with the text. Sixteenth-century Christian humanist and biblical scholar Erasmus points out the value of active reading:

> I consider as lovers of books, not those who keep their books hidden in their store-chests and never handle them, but those who, by nightly as well as daily use, thumb them, batter them, wear them out, who fill out all the margins with annotations of many kinds, and who prefer the marks of a fault they have erased to a neat copy full of faults.[5]

A book full of marks is like an intellectual diary. It shows your engagement with the author. Mortimer Adler unpacks the process of marking a book in his 1941 article for the *Saturday Review of Literature* aptly titled "How to Mark a Book."[6] While technology sometimes changes the way we read, it is still important to "mark" what you read. It may take the form of electronically highlighting, typing notes, or using a stylus. Whatever form you use, you should seek to intentionally engage with the text, leaving yourself signposts to which you can return to find the thesis, major points, compelling statements, key terms, and questions you have. You can do this by underlining, highlighting, circling, or making notes in the margins.

Let's examine in greater depth the key questions connected with discerning the theologian's view.

---

5. Desiderius Erasmus, *Correspondence*, vol. 1 in *Collected Works of Erasmus*, ed. Richard J. Schoeck and Beatrice Corrigan (Toronto: University of Toronto Press, 1974), 58.

6. This article can be found in Audrey Fielding and Ruth Schoenbach, eds., *Building Academic Literacy: An Anthology for Reading Apprenticeship* (San Francisco: Jossey-Bass, 2003), 179–84.

THE MAIN CONTENTION: WHAT IS THE THEOLOGIAN CONTENDING IN THE WORK?

The aim, contention, or "argument" of a work, which generally appears in the introduction or early on in the book, is what the author holds to be true and seeks to convey to the reader. We often associate the word *argument* with a disagreement or debate. While the "argument" can include that, as is the case with Erasmus and Luther in their works on the nature of the will respectively titled *Freedom of the Will* and *Bondage of the Will*, the term is not limited to a debate. Instead, we should understand this term as a technical term related to critical thinking.[7]

A theological argument is comprised of two parts: the thesis and the key arguments explaining why it is deemed to be true. Let's look more closely at these two components.

WHAT IS THE THESIS OF THE WORK?

The word *thesis* derives from the Greek word *tithenai* that means "to put something forth." A thesis statement is the central claim or proposition that the theologian is putting forward in the text. This core claim stands as the organizing principle of the work. It serves as the theologian's response to a crucial question or theme. Most often a thesis statement is associated with academic works, yet it can also be found in subtler forms of works such as poems, novels, and even confessions. A good thesis statement goes beyond just discussing a topic or giving a personal perspective. It offers an informed opinion that the author intends to support with evidence, whether by facts, biblical evidence, or experience.

When you identify the thesis, it is helpful to underline or make a vertical line in the margin of the work. For example,

---

7. See, for example, Simon Blackburn, *The Oxford Dictionary of Philosophy*, 3rd ed. (Oxford: Oxford University Press, 2016), 29, which defines an argument as: "To argue is to produce considerations designed to support a conclusion."

John Milton provides the main argument of *Paradise Lost*, the epic poem about the biblical account of the fall of mankind, in the opening lines:

> *Of man's first disobedience, and the fruit*
> *Of that forbidden tree, whose mortal taste*
> *Brought death into the world, and all our woe,*
> *With loss of Eden, till one greater Man*
> *Restore us, and regain the blissful seat.*[8]

The poem was written, in his own words, that "I may assert Eternal Providence, and justify the ways of God to men."[9] The rest of the poem develops Milton's argument about God's just providence and human culpability in the fall.

To help confirm that you have understood the author's main contention, you should be able to concisely restate the thesis in your own words, being careful not to interject your opinion of the work. Milton's thesis, for instance, could be restated as "Adam's disobedience by choosing the forbidden fruit over God is to blame for the loss of Paradise." The restatement of the thesis should preserve the original meaning of the text, showing that you accurately understand the author's position. The more clearly and concisely you can paraphrase the thesis without changing its meaning, the better. Mortimer Adler points out that "the person who says he knows what he thinks but cannot express it usually does not know what he thinks."[10] This same statement can be applied to an undiscerning reader. Accurately restating the author's main contention in one's own words helps to solidify the reader's understanding of the author's intent.

---

8. John Milton, *Paradise Lost* (Chicago: Thompson and Thomas, 1901), 9.

9. Milton, *Paradise Lost*, 10.

10. Adler, *How to Read a Book*, 49.

WHAT ARE THE KEY POINTS?

The second part of an argument is the set of reasons or critical points that the theologian offers in support of his or her thesis. In learning how to identify the key points, it is helpful to look beyond the section dividers, topic headings, the questions being asked by the author, and key phrases. While it is beneficial to identify and "mark" them, this information is not sufficient for determining the key points. In fact, without further investigation, this information alone can be misunderstood and lead the reader to think that the author is supporting a view that he or she may actually be dialoguing with or refuting. Instead, the reader should seek to identify the primary evidence the author gives in support of the thesis.

For instance, John Milton divides the 1674 version of *Paradise Lost* into twelve books, helping the reader identify some of the major themes in each book: man's disobedience, the role of Satan, God's divine foreknowledge, the battles of Satan, God's warning, the creation of the world, the creation of man, Adam and Eve's relationship, the temptation by Satan, the Son as judge, the Son as intercessor, the loss of Paradise, and the comfort of God's promise. If one were only to identify these themes and not the propositions, one might wrongly interpret Milton as suggesting that Satan, not God, is the hero of the epic. It is accurate to acknowledge that Satan has a prominent role in the poem. When the key points are identified, however, it is quickly evident that he is not the hero.

Milton justifies God's ways with several points: the importance of obedience to God, the natural hierarchy of the universe, asserting God's divine foreknowledge and providence; showing the connection between free will and disobedience; pointing to how the fall positively reveals God's grace, mercy, and justice; and showing how God provides redemption and hope through his Son. Whenever you identify a key point, it is helpful to make a note in the margin or on a separate document, listing each key point in order. This will help you understand how the author develops and supports his or her thesis.

UNDERSTANDING THEOLOGICAL TERMS: WHAT ARE THE KEY TERMS?

Understanding the author's key terms is essential in order to truly comprehend a theological text. It is crucial to understand the terms in the way the author is using them. Whenever possible, one should avoid using a dictionary, even a theological dictionary, to define the key terms, since the author may not be using the word according to a dictionary's definition. While outside resources may be helpful to understand some of the general terms, it is equally essential to know how an author is using their key terms.[11] The essential terms help unpack the arguments being presented.

The assumption that all authors use vocabulary in the same conventional way can be an especially dangerous pitfall, especially when one is reading a theological work that has a different context from one's own. One only needs to order "chips" in both an American restaurant and an English pub to recognize how a common word can mean two very different things depending on the context. This is often the case with theological texts, whether reading a translation or a work written in a different historical, ecclesiastical, social, or intellectual setting. Even when works are written in the same apparent setting, various authors can ascribe different meanings to the same word.

---

11. For general terms, where it is not essential to know how the author is using the word, one can consult resources such as Justo L. González, *Essential Theological Terms* (Louisville, KY: Westminster John Knox, 2005); William A. Dyrness and Veli-Matti Kärkkäinen, eds., *Global Dictionary of Theology: A Resource for the Worldwide Church* (Downers Grove, IL: IVP Academic, 2008); Donald K. McKim, *Westminster Dictionary of Theological Terms* (Louisville, KY: Westminster John Knox, 1996); and Stanley J. Grenz, David Guretzki, and Cherith Fee Nordling, *Pocket Dictionary of Theological Terms* (Downers Grove, IL: InterVarsity, 1999).

The word *evangelical* exemplifies the importance of understanding the author's definition of a key term. The term *evangelical* is derived from the Greek word *euangelion*, which means "gospel" or "good news." If you were to look it up in *Merriam-Webster*'s dictionary, you would find the following definitions:[12]

> **1** : of, relating to, or being in agreement with the Christian gospel esp. as it is presented in the four Gospels **2** : PROTESTANT **3** : emphasizing salvation by faith in the atoning death of Jesus Christ through personal conversion, the authority of Scripture, and the importance of preaching as contrasted with ritual **4** : **a** *cap* : of or relating to the Evangelical Church in Germany **b** *often cap* : of, adhering to, or marked by fundamentalism: FUNDAMENTALIST **c** *often cap* : LOW CHURCH **5** : marked by militant or crusading zeal: EVANGELISTIC

Which of these definitions, if any, is correct? The word *evangelical* can have a very different meaning, depending on who is using it and in what context. The dictionary on its own is not sufficient to help one discern how an author is using this word.

The term was first used by Sir Thomas More in 1531 to refer to advocates of the Reformation. As late as the eighteenth century, it was used in the general sense to refer to "of the gospel." In 1723, Isaac Watts, for instance, wrote of an "Evangelical Turn of Thought."[13]

The term *Evangelical* with an uppercase letter began to be used regularly in the 1730s to refer to any aspect of the Protestant movement.[14] Historian David Bebbington points out that after this point, however, the term *Evangelical* began

---

12. "Evangelical," *Merriam-Webster*, www.merriam-webster.com/dictionary/evangelical.
13. Cited in D. W. Bebbington, *Evangelicalism in Modern Britain: A History from the 1730s to the 1980s* (New York: Routledge, 2015), 1.
14. See Bebbington, *Evangelicalism in Modern Britain*, 1.

to be characterized by four necessary marks: conversionism (the belief that lives need to be changed), activism (the expression of the gospel in effort), biblicism (high regard for the Bible), and crucicentrism (stress on the sacrifice of Christ on the cross).[15]

In the late nineteenth century, the term became associated more closely with "biblicism." Then in the twentieth century, the "Evangelical" movement became associated with a conversion experience. So how should we understand the term? While many theologians identify themselves as "Evangelical," they often mean radically different things. The late Christian blogger and writer Rachel Held Evans, for instance, formerly identified herself as an "Evangelical" while appearing to question the ultimate authority of Scripture and the exclusivity of the cross, two of Bebbington's essential marks.[16] So to truly understand what someone means by the word *evangelical*, we must examine specifically how they use it.

How do we go about discovering which words are key terms? Obviously, not all words are equally important in a text. We only need to focus on words that have special significance to the meaning of the work and that if misunderstood would change the meaning of the text or hinder the apprehension of it.

---

15. See "What Is an Evangelical?" National Association of Evangelicals, https:// www.nae.net/what-is-an-evangelical. Bebbington unpacks these marks in his book *Evangelicalism in Modern Britain: A History from the 1730s to the 1930s*, 2–19.

16. See, for example, her book *Inspired: Slaying Giants, Walking on Water, and Loving the Bible Again* (Nashville: Nelson, 2018), where she wrote, "My aim with this book is to recapture of that Bible magic, but in a way that honors the text for what it is—ancient, complicated, debated, and untidy, both universally relevant and born from a specific context and culture . . . I hope to show that the Bible can be captivating and true when taken on its own terms, avoiding both strict literalism on the one hand and safe, disinterested liberalism on the other" (pp. xxi–xxii). She discusses why she does not hold the Bible as fully authoritative or Christianity as exclusive in the following blog posts: "Have We Made the Bible into an Idol?" May 13, 2008, https://rachelheldevans.com /blog/article-1210736874; "Biblical Considerations for an Inclusive View of Salvation," November 16, 2010, https://rachelheldevans.com/blog/bible -inclusive-salvation-heaven-hell. More recently, she had moved away from her "Evangelical" identity, which she wrote about in her book *Searching for Sunday: Loving, Leaving, and Finding the Church* (Nashville: Nelson, 2015).

You should begin by determining the meaning of words that are unfamiliar to you. Many of these words are often used according to the common understanding. It is important, however, to not assume that, but rather to confirm its usage by examining the text. If you don't know the word *Apocrypha*, for example, you can look it up in almost any dictionary and discover it refers to a set of fourteen ancient texts that are included between the Old and New Testaments in the *Vulgate* (a fourth-century Latin translation of the Bible) and in Roman Catholic Bibles. While not all unfamiliar words are crucial to the argument of the text, you should still seek to understand them, since they will help you comprehend what you are reading.

Once you have identified unfamiliar words, it is important to discover the key terms. These are words or phrases that help communicate presuppositions, essential ideas, or support the arguments of the text. One way to begin to identify a key term is by examining terms that are intentionally stressed in the text. Look for words that are set in bold or italics, encased in quotes, placed in a bigger font, underlined, emphasized repeatedly, or explicitly defined in the text. These are usually indicators that the author or publisher recognizes their significance.

Another way to identify key terms is to examine the author's thesis and supporting points. Do they contain essential terms? Additionally, one should look for words that the author uses in a unique way in the text. Theologians, especially German ones, are infamous for using obscure, ambiguous, or even inventive terminology, often coining new terms. For example, the words *Trinity, Eucharist, original sin, total depravity,* and *inerrancy* do not appear in the Bible, nor are they popular words in mainstream English. Yet many theologians have come to accept these terms as crucial to the Christian faith.

Even a seemingly simple word like *will* can be a key term. This term, for instance, is critical to both Luther's and Erasmus's theology, though they understand it in radically different ways.

In *Bondage of the Will*, Luther understood the will to be corrupt, sinful, and unable to please God without God's grace. In contrast, in *Freedom of the Will*, Erasmus saw the will as the voluntary power by which a human can apply oneself to the things that lead to eternal life. If this term is not properly understood, each author's perspective on the human condition would not be clear.

As illustrated earlier, using dictionaries may be helpful for defining unfamiliar words in the text, but readers can be confused or misled when they use them to discern the meaning of key terms apart from considering the author's intended meaning. As with the thesis and key arguments, it is helpful to articulate the author's usage of the key terms in your own words, being careful to retain the author's understanding. This will help confirm your comprehension of the terms.

PUTTING IT ALL TOGETHER: AN EXAMPLE OF DISCERNING AN AUTHOR'S VIEW

Is the Bible free from error or fault? If not, to what extent do errors prevail? Biblical inerrancy is a hotly debated topic among Evangelicals, as the Bible is central to the Evangelical faith and identity. For many Evangelicals, biblical inerrancy is the core identifying principle. The book *Five Views on Biblical Inerrancy* examines "the current spectrum of evangelical opinion" on inerrancy.[17]

When reading this book, you will quickly discover that while each author broadly identifies himself as an "Evangelical," each holds a different perspective regarding biblical inerrancy. All the authors agree that "God graciously accommodates himself to human sensibilities," yet they "diverge when considering the manner, degree, and extent to which he does."[18] While two scholars, Michael Bird and Peter Enns, suggest that the concept

---

17. Stanley N. Gundry, J. Merrick, and Stephen M. Garrett, eds., *Five Views on Biblical Inerrancy* (Grand Rapids: Zondervan, 2013), 23.

18. Gundry, Merrick, and Garrett, eds., *Five Views on Biblical Inerrancy*, 318.

should be abandoned, the other three—Albert Mohler, Kevin Vanhoozer, and John Franke—support its continued use, though each holds a variant perspective on biblical inerrancy.

If one were to read this book assuming that each author is using *Merriam-Webster*'s definition of *Evangelical* and *inerrancy*, one would not be able to discern the nuances of each perspective.[19] It is only when each author's thesis, key points, and key terms are identified that one can truly ascertain how each answers the question, "What is the significance of the doctrine of inerrancy?"

Enns and Mohler center their arguments around the historical nature of the doctrine of inerrancy and its place in shaping Evangelical identity. Enns seeks to point out the flaws in older views of inerrancy, while Mohler supports a "classic inerrantist" perspective, aligning himself with Evangelical forerunners of the concept such as B. B. Warfield, Carl Henry, and the Chicago Statement on Biblical Inerrancy.

In contrast, Australian scholar Michael Bird, while supporting the concept of inerrancy, contends that it is "parochially American in context" and imposes an alien terminology on Scripture. Instead, he suggests using the concepts of the "*infallibility* and *authority* of Scripture."[20] Similarly, Kevin Vanhoozer affirms the concept but proposes what he calls a "well-versed inerrancy" that functions to humble the reader under the text.[21]

The final author, John Franke, a self-professed "post-conservative" Evangelical, recommends a "recasting" of inerrancy that sees the Bible as "witness to missional plurality." His chapter portrays the truth of the Word of God as an event tied to the Holy Spirit's work rather than a proposition.[22]

---

19. *Merriam-Webster* defines *inerrancy* as "exemption from error" (www .merriam-webster.com/dictionary/inerrancy).

20. Gundry, Merrick, and Garrett, eds., *Five Views on Biblical Inerrancy*, 145–46.

21. Gundry, Merrick, and Garrett, eds., *Five Views on Biblical Inerrancy*, 204.

22. Gundry, Merrick, and Garrett, eds., *Five Views on Biblical Inerrancy*, 259, 270–73, 276.

Each author's argument in this book attempts to persuade Evangelical readers how they should understand the truthfulness and purpose of God's Word. The range of perspectives on *inerrancy* can only be understood and evaluated when one listens well to each author's arguments. As Mortimer Adler rightly says, "Successful communication occurs in any case where what the writer wanted to have received finds its way into the reader's possession."[23]

CONCLUSION

As the Greek philosopher Epictetus asserted, "We have two ears and one mouth so we can listen twice as much as we speak."[24] Unfortunately, we often value our mouth more than our ears. With a social media-saturated culture that inspires individuals to "speak their minds," it can be challenging to listen well. Yet Scripture implores us to do just that. Proverbs 20:12 helps us recognize that God created us with "the hearing ear and the seeing eye."

How do we listen well to the authors we read? Not by leaving books with clean pages and unbroken bindings. Instead, we need to truly engage with them, seeking to listen for the author's argument before responding. Erasmus of Rotterdam describes book lovers as doing just that.

If we want to discern the truths contained in theological works, we must identify the author's thesis, key points, and critical terms so that we can truly comprehend the argument set forth. Our inability to discern is often linked to our failure to genuinely listen to the author so that we can hear his or her message. If we cannot repeat back in our own words the author's argument, then we probably have not truly listened.

---

23. Adler, *How to Read a Book*, 6.
24. Cited in Holmes, "9 Things Good Listeners Do Differently."

QUESTIONS FOR DISCUSSION AND REFLECTION

1. Good communication, namely, communication that involves active listening and being open to considering another person's perspective, is an essential element of true friendship and wisdom. Reading theology well, like active listening, is an art that requires work, skill, and attentiveness. What are some of the things that keep you from listening well to a theologian?

2. Erasmus of Rotterdam wrote, "I consider as lovers of books, not those who keep their books hidden in their store-chests and never handle them, but those who, by nightly as well as daily use, thumb them, batter them, wear them out, who fill out all the margins with annotations of many kinds, and who prefer the marks of a fault they have erased to a neat copy full of faults." Would Erasmus consider you a "lover of books"? What does the condition of your books reveal about your reading practices?

3. A book full of marks is like an intellectual diary, revealing the engagement of the reader with the text. List three practical takeaways from this chapter to help you more effectively keep an "intellectual diary" in the theological works you read.

4. The word *argument* is often understood as a derogatory term relating to an adversarial frame of mind. What is a theological argument generally comprised of? How can it differ from the derogatory use of the term?

5. It is common to confuse a theological theme or question with a theologian's thesis statement. What is the difference between the two? What makes a good thesis statement?

6. This chapter warns against seeing section dividers or headings in a theological work as key points. Why? How do they differ?

7. Understanding the author's key terms is essential to truly apprehending a theological text. Give an example of a common word that if misunderstood changes the meaning of what's being communicated.

8. Mortimer Adler insists that the "person who says he knows what he thinks but cannot express it usually does not know what he thinks." How can we apply this statement to reading? What practical steps could you take with the next theological work you read to express that you have listened well to the text?

9. Greek philosopher Epictetus asserted that "we have two ears and one mouth so we can listen twice as much as we speak." Name one way you can seek to listen more actively this week both in your reading and in your communication with others.

PRACTICE DISCERNING THE THEOLOGIAN'S VIEW

What is the theologian seeking to communicate?

1. Briefly examine a theological work and answer the following questions:
   - What is the theologian contending in the work?
   - What is the thesis of the work? Concisely restate the thesis in your own words. (One or two sentences is ideal.)
   - What are the key points of the theological work? Concisely restate them in your own words.

2. What are the key terms that are important in understanding the theologian's perspective?
   - Identify and define the words in the text you don't know.
   - Identify and define the words important to the theologian's arguments.

3. What does all this information tell you about what the theologian is seeking to communicate?

CHAPTER 8

Assessing: Evaluating and Applying the Theological Work

Doctrine forms disciples when it helps the church to act out its new life in Christ.

KEVIN VANHOOZER,
FAITH SPEAKING UNDERSTANDING

Do not be conformed to this world, but be transformed by the renewal of your mind, that by testing you may discern what is the will of God, what is good and acceptable and perfect.

ROMANS 12:2

What is the value of the work?

How are judgments made? We may think our judgments are based on rational thought. Scientific research, however, suggests otherwise. Think about a job interview, for example. You may have spent many hours preparing for it, but before you even shake hands, your potential employer may have already decided whether or not to hire you. This decision was probably not based on your résumé, references, or anything you said. More likely, it hinged on the interviewer's first impression of you.

Studies reveal that even when we have already gathered a lot of information, a first impression or an intuition is often the primary driving factor in the decisions we make. We are constantly making judgments. Our snap judgments can affect who we hire, vote for, or even date. Think back to chapter 1 where we considered the Getty Museum's decision of whether or not to purchase a supposedly ancient Greek *kouros* sculpture. First impressions matter, even for experts. Our natural intuition can properly guide us or mislead us. This is true even in issues of faith. That is why it is so important to take time to identify our biases and initial assessments and be willing to reappraise them, seeking to train our minds and hearts to discern what is true and good (Romans 12:2).

This principle applies to our assessment of theological works. Current culture often communicates negative messages about judging, encouraging people to become more accepting of other religious perspectives. Even among Christians, Matthew 7 is often cited as a reason to not judge others' beliefs. When it comes to theological works, however, Scripture is clear that we are to discern the truth from false teaching (Luke 6:43–45; Acts 20:28; 1 John 4). Furthermore, whether we intend to or not, from the moment we pick up a book, we are assessing it. The real question we should be asking, however, is, *How* are we to judge it? In other words, How can we spot the genuine *kouros* from the forgery? Or in the case of theology, How can we spot the truth?

Your assessment of the value of a work should not be merely a matter of uneducated snap judgments, personal opinions, or subjective preferences. The previous chapters have laid out a plan for careful inspection of a work, with the goal of training you to *ask* the right kinds of questions and guide you in *how* to discover the answers. Through the process of examining the textual features, the context, the theological framework, the sources, and the theologian's views, you will have a better picture of *what* the author is actually communicating.

Examining a work should be similar to taking the time to get to know a person by listening to her thoughts, asking clarifying questions, and accurately hearing her responses. Once the hard work of careful inspection is done and you have become acquainted with the theological work, you are in a better position to more fully, accurately, and responsively evaluate it and recognize its value.

It should be noted that the value of a theological work does not merely rest in how readable it is or how closely it aligns with one's own beliefs. Ultimately, its value rests in how it moves you toward truly knowing and loving God and others (Matthew 22:36–40). Sometimes this happens when the work points you toward truth, and sometimes when it helps point out flaws in your thinking, illuminates difficult doctrines, clarifies concepts, or makes you aware of the dangers of holding unbiblical beliefs. The following steps can train your mind and heart to properly assess the theological works you read:

- Continue to pray for discernment.
- Test and evaluate the text against Scripture.
- Determine the practical significance of the ideas in the text.
- Discover the value of the work and its implications.

While we should pray, test, and seek to understand a text and to discover the value, implications, and practical application of a work throughout the reading process, the final appraisal of a work should happen after the initial questions have been thoroughly addressed. This process will help correct hasty, unfounded judgments, whether they are positive or negative. The appraisal process allows us to prayerfully and logically reexamine a text. Or as Kevin Vanhoozer puts it, "Doctrine forms disciples when it helps the church to act out its new life in Christ."[1]

BEGINNING THE REAPPRAISAL PROCESS

Before one can wisely agree or disagree with someone, one must also be sure he or she has adequately understood what has been said. As Mortimer Adler puts it, "To agree without understanding is inane. To disagree without understanding is impudent."[2] Judging a work before prayerfully reading it while using the tools of discernment is like giving an opinion of a food without having tasted it. Imagine asking a person who lacks a sense of taste to write a restaurant review. In order to be a qualified food critic, one has to have not only a sense of taste but also a developed palate. Once the hard work of careful inspection is done, a reader is in a better position, like the qualified food critic, to evaluate the value of the work.

When you begin your reappraisal, remember to prayerfully seek God's counsel. Prayer acknowledges our dependence on God for knowing the truth and living it out. The practice of prayer invites the Holy Spirit into the discernment process. In your reappraisal, you also should review the information you have already gathered.

Here are a few helpful questions that can direct you in the reappraisal process:

---

1. Kevin J. Vanhoozer, *Faith Speaking Understanding: Performing the Drama of Doctrine* (Louisville, KY: Westminster John Knox, 2014), 6.
2. Mortimer J. Adler and Charles Van Doren, *How to Read a Book* (New York: Simon & Schuster, 1972), 143.

- How does the theologian's background, presuppositions, context, and audience inform the theological ideas of the text?
- What impact does the theological framework have on the theological ideas of the text?
- How does the theologian's use of sources impact his or her interpretation of Scripture?
- How well does the theologian support his or her theological views?

Reviewing the text with this information in mind will help prepare you to evaluate the text more accurately and to avoid basing your assessment on erroneous snap judgments.

GOING DEEPER IN THE EVALUATION PROCESS
What is the coherency, veracity, and significance of the text?

Having begun the reappraisal process by reviewing the work, you can prayerfully move toward fully evaluating the work. Evaluating a work is more like writing a book review than a book report. While book reports are helpful in summarizing the content, they generally lack a critical and practical evaluation of the work. While a report may contain some personal opinions about a book, generally it lacks an in-depth analysis of the work. To move beyond merely reporting on a theological work, one must make a more in-depth investigation of its *coherency*, *veracity*, and *significance*. Each of these categories will be expounded on below.

Coherency
How coherent is the theological text?

Coherence is the condition of internal consistency. In other words, something is coherent when it makes sense on a fundamental level. A coherent argument is one that is communicated in a cogent manner. It is clear, logical, complete, consistent, and understandable. "All bachelors are unmarried" is a coherent statement. It is both understandable and logical. Similarly, well-written theological texts should be coherent. They should clearly and intelligibly communicate theological views and support them. Coherency is a matter of both structure and content. When evaluating a theological work for coherency, you are seeking to determine how well the author communicates his or her views.

Here are some questions to help assess a theological work's coherency:

- How intelligible is the theological work?
- How clear and consistent are the theologian's contentions?
- How well-defined are the key terms in the text?
- How well does the theologian support his or her contentions?

In assessing the coherency of a theological work, it is important to remember that you are looking at the proficiency with which the author communicates theological knowledge. At this stage, you are not focusing on evaluating the truthfulness of the work. A work can be intelligible and have clear and consistent contentions, well-defined key terms, and logical support, and yet still be false. The reverse may also be true. A theologian may cryptically communicate his or her views and lack clear support, yet still speak truth.

For instance, the following argument is logically invalid, yet the conclusion is true:

1. God created the heavens and the earth.
2. God delivered his people from Egypt.
3. Therefore Jesus died for the sins of the world.

While the premises (#1 and #2) and conclusion (#3) are correct, the conclusion does not follow from the premises.

By contrast, one could make the following *valid* argument in which the conclusion is *false*:

1. All humans are sinful.
2. Jesus is a human.
3. Therefore Jesus is sinful.

While this argument is logically valid (the conclusion follows from the premises), it is nonetheless false. Biblically, the first two premises are correct. However, the conclusion is errant. As Scripture testifies, all humans are sinful (Romans 3:23), and Jesus was fully human (Galatians 4:4), yet Jesus was born without sin and never sinned (Hebrews 4:15). Thus the presence or a lack of logical structure doesn't indicate by itself whether a theologian's arguments are true or false.

Many significant theological works lack full coherency but are nonetheless valuable sources of truth. For instance, *Interior Castle*, the mystical work by Saint Teresa of Avila, lacks a logical structure and clear definitions but still serves a valuable purpose in pointing people toward prayerful contemplation and intimacy with Christ. It is still necessary, however, to consider how coherent a theological work is. The coherency of a theological work helps the reader access the ideas contained within it.

Veracity
How truthful is the work?

God and God's words are always true (John 17:17). Unfortunately, the same cannot be said about humans, even godly humans. As Numbers 23:19 rightly proclaims, "God is not man, that he should lie, or a son of man, that he should change his mind. Has he said, and will he not do it? Or has he spoken, and will he not fulfill it?" Scripture warns us to not believe every theologian

(Matthew 7:15; 24:4–5; 1 John 4:1). Even those who desire to uphold God's truth can err. Good motives are not sufficient.

It is essential, therefore, to prayerfully test all of a theologian's ideas against biblical truth. As Peter proclaims, Scripture is God's Word that is carried along by the Holy Spirit. It is not "cleverly devised myths" (2 Peter 1:16). Biblical veracity should be the primary criteria for evaluating a theological work. It is also vital to examine a work's logical veracity.

Here are some questions that help discern the veracity of a theological text:

- **Are the theologian's presuppositions true?** Examine how biblical the author's presuppositions are and how they impact the work.
- **Are the ideas derived from or consistent with Scripture?** Examine the text to discover whether the author is asserting biblical truths or merely proof-texting or expressing ideas inconsistent with Scripture.
- **How sufficiently does the theologian support his or her views?** Assess whether the ideas are based merely on personal opinion or subjective experience, or whether they are rooted in God's Word or other objective means.
- **Are the author's arguments logically valid?** Consider whether they are logically valid arguments that contain true premises that lead to true conclusions.
- **Do the tone and the content of the text exhibit the wisdom of the Spirit or the spirit of worldliness?** Look at whether the text exhibits spiritual wisdom (Colossians 1:9–10) and the fruit of the Spirit (love, joy, peace, patience, kindness, goodness, faithfulness, gentleness, self-control; Galatians 5:22–25) that glorify God or, in contrast, worldliness and sin (such as conceit, provoking one another, envy; Galatians 5:19–25) that are hostile to God and do not submit to God's law (Romans 8:3).

These questions can help guide your evaluation. It is essential to keep in mind, however, that the truthfulness of a work is not dependent on the type of work or even whether it directly cites Scripture. A poem that is loosely based on Scripture, for instance, can be more faithful to biblical truth than an exegetical work. A comparison of George Herbert's poem "Love (III)" and Mary Baker Eddy's exposition of Genesis exemplifies this point. Below is Herbert's poem:

> *Love bade me welcome; yet my soul drew back,*
>   *Guilty of dust and sin.*
> *But quick-eyed Love, observing me grow slack*
>   *From my first entrance in,*
> *Drew nearer to me, sweetly questioning*
>   *If I lack'd any thing.*
>
> *A guest, I answer'd, worthy to be here:*
>   *Love said, You shall be he.*
> *I, the unkind, ungrateful? Ah, my dear,*
>   *I cannot look on thee.*
> *Love took my hand, and smiling did reply,*
>   *Who made the eyes but I?*
>
> *Truth, Lord, but I have marr'd them: let my shame*
>   *Go where it doth deserve.*
> *And know you not, says Love, who bore the blame?*
>   *My dear, then I will serve.*
> *You must sit down, says Love, and taste my meat:*
>   *So I did sit and eat.*[3]

While at first glance this poem does not appear to be based on a biblical passage, it actually echoes Luke 12:37 (KJV),

---

3. George Herbert, *The Poetical Works of George Herbert* (Edinburgh: Nichol, 1857), 200.

which contains the phrase "he shall . . . make them to sit down to meat." As Chana Block rightly points out, "The Bible provides the means" for Herbert "by which an experience is translated into words and given poetic form. The subject is conceived biblically, as it were, and expressed biblically: the dramatic situation, the images, the tension of ideas, the very shape of the plot, all have their source in the Bible."[4]

Herbert's poem unpacks the scriptural portrayal of the love of God displayed in God's invitation to the sinner to eat with him. His use of the biblical metaphor of a feast (found in Song of Solomon 2:4; Isaiah 25:6–9; Matthew 22:1–14; etc.) also recalls the narrative of the prodigal son in Luke 15:11–32, where the gracious father welcomes the rebellious son home and lavishes his unconditional love on him. In an experiential manner, Herbert paints a picture of the biblical truths of human depravity and shame and the opportunity for the sinner to accept God's mercy, grace, and love.

Herbert's poetry is full of biblical truths. In contrast, Mary Baker Eddy's Scripture-packed sermons and writings are full of heretical ideas. The founder of Christian Science claims that the Bible is the only authority, yet she contradictorily upholds her divine revelation as a primary source of truth and often gives her own spiritualized interpretations of biblical passages. Her "scientific revelations" recorded in the book *Science and Health* serve as the "key" to understanding the Scriptures.

This approach is evident in her understanding of the creation of humankind in the book of Genesis. She insisted that while the first chapter of Genesis correctly described humanity as created in the image of God, the second chapter was a "false history in contradistinction to the true." She asserted that Genesis 2, "which portrays Spirit as supposedly cooperating with matter in constructing the universe, is based on some hypothesis of error."

---

4. Chana Bloch, "George Herbert and the Bible: A Reading of 'Love (III),'" *English Literary Renaissance* 8, no. 3 (Autumn 1978): 329–40.

Her understanding of Genesis questioned the manner of the creation, the fall, and even the need for salvation, as evidenced in her rhetorical question: "Does Life, Truth, and Love produce death, error, and hatred? Does the creator condemn His own creation?"[5] Instead, she claimed that the only hope of pardon and salvation for any person lies in that person eliminating all sin (false beliefs and the behavior they spawn) from his or her life.[6]

When one compares the teachings of Eddy to Herbert, it is evident that Scripture references are not enough to make a work biblical or true. The ideas must be derived from or be consistent with Scripture. Scripture is the best interpreter of itself, not personal "scientific revelations."

Furthermore, it is crucial to recognize that even if a theological text or an idea is not directly derived from Scripture, it may still contain truth. For instance, in *Still Following Christ in a Consumer Society*, Jesuit priest John Kavanaugh makes important critiques regarding the negative influence that the consumer culture has had on the church and the world.

While Scripture is the source of truth and the final authority in matters of truth, some truths can be known naturally through God's common grace. As Scripture proclaims, "The heavens declare the glory of God, and the sky above proclaims his handiwork" (Psalm 19:1). These truths, however, cannot contradict God's revelation in the Word. Everything should be tested against Scripture (1 Thessalonians 5:21).

SIGNIFICANCE

What is the significance of the theological ideas/principles in the text?

The prior steps of reading theology have primarily focused on factual, conceptual, and critical inquiry. Examining the

---

5. Mary Baker Eddy, *Science and Health with Key to the Scriptures* (1875; repr., Boston: Christian Science Board of Directors, 2006), 522.

6. See Eddy, *Science and Health*, 40.

significance of a theological work, however, moves beyond these modes of investigation toward a more practical mode of inquiry. Engaging in this mode of investigation goes beyond reading for facts, meaning, coherency, veracity, or even determining the credibility of a work. Theological texts can be both coherent and true, yet not be profitable for the Christian faith and practice. Therefore, it is vital to assess the significance of a theological work, seeking to discover its practical and spiritual value.

Below are some of the questions that can help unpack the significance of a work:

- **How does this theological work impact our view of God, ourselves, and our understanding of the world?** Examine how it leads people to true knowledge of God, humanity, and the world.
- **What is the significance of the theological ideas for the individual, the church, and the world?** Seek to determine how the message of the text can be applied to the original and the current context.
- **How does the theological text point to Christ and advance the gospel?** Examine whether the work helps awaken sinners to believe and abide in Christ
- **How spiritually beneficial or harmful are the ideas in the text?** Look at whether it encourages spiritual growth and how it prepares people for Christian worship and service of God.
- **By what principles does the text encourage Christians today to live?** Examine whether or not the principles it advocates are biblical.

In the evaluative process, it is essential to recognize that the value of a work does not merely rest on whether one agrees with it, or even whether it is rooted in Scripture. One should also consider whether or not it compels the reader to right thinking, godly living, and appropriate worship of God. Engaging with texts that may even challenge aspects of the Christian faith or practice can be a valuable exercise.

For instance, Friedrich Nietzsche, one of the most infamous critics of Christianity, rejects the truthfulness of the Christian faith; however, the questions he raises regarding free will, morality, and the value of religion still hold practical importance for the Christian reader. Practical inquiry enables the reader to engage with thinkers like Nietzsche on a deeper level, recognizing the value of their perspective, even if their views differ. The evaluative process requires the reader to go beyond critical thinking, where one primarily listens in order to critique a text, and instead to seek to engage theologians in a more conversant manner.

When one attempts to determine the significance of the work, one should ask what growth can come from engaging with the text. This type of inquiry will be further discussed in the next section on the application of theological writings.

Practical Significance
What are the practical implications and possible applications of this work?

Reading theology should never be an end in and of itself. If the purpose of reading theology is not worldly knowledge but godly wisdom or, as John Calvin puts it, "knowledge of God and of ourselves,"[7] then it is not enough to read theology simply for understanding or even for evaluative purposes. We should also seek to discover the practical significance of a theological text regarding our view of God, ourselves, and the world we inhabit.

Discovering the practical implications and applications of theological ideas is foundational for Christian growth.

---

7. *Inst.*, I.1.1.

Theology is to not only be understood but also lived. The purpose of theology is to gain true knowledge that leads to proper worship, spiritual renewal, and faithful service. As Kelly Kapic correctly assesses, "There is no such thing as a disembodied theology. All theology is lived . . . There is this inescapable back-and-forth dynamic that exists between our experiences and our thinking." Where theology really matters is "in the midst of real people and real circumstances."[8] Therefore it is vital to ask the question, *So what?* In other words, what are the practical implications and applications of what is being communicated in the theological text?

Let's further expound on this idea with the following questions:

- **What are the practical implications of the theological work for the individual, the church, and society?** Identify the consequences or results associated with holding the views and putting them into practice.
- **How is the theological work relevant to the problems and challenges that the average person or church faces?** In other words, examine how the theological ideas relate to real life.
- **What kind of impact do the theological ideas have on the church's identity and practices?** Examine how the ideas practically impact worship, evangelism, ministry, and service.
- **How does this work practically contribute to the love of God and neighbor (Matthew 22:37–39)?** Notice how it practically compels you to love God and others through the power of the Holy Spirit.

---

8. Cited in Richard Doster, "Practical Theology: Our Interview with Dr. Kelly M. Kapic," *By Faith*, January 14, 2013, https://byfaithonline.com/practical-theology.

- **How does this work practically compel one to maturity in Christ (Colossians 1:28)?** Determine which ideas are spiritually enriching and should be appropriated and which should be discarded or even refuted.
- **How do the ideas contribute to the world becoming what God intends it to be?** Discern how the ideas can and be can't be used to practically transform the world in accordance with God's will for creation.
- **How does the work clarify, illuminate, or defend biblical and theological truths, either today or in the history of the church?** Examine how the work helps you to understand or express theological truths.
- **Does the work help me understand a viewpoint, idea, or movement that may be significant even if not theologically orthodox?** How might the work deepen your understanding or comprehension of theology.

These questions are meant to help us discern the practical benefits of dialoguing with theological texts. One can see the importance of this process when reading Medieval Scholastic theology. Many contemporary readers often struggle to see the value of Scholastic theology due to its abstract, theoretical nature that tends to offer fewer direct implications for faith and daily life.

One only needs to examine Anselm's lengthy digression about angels in *Cur Deus Homo*? (*Why God Became Man*) to see why Scholastic theology has been criticized as impractical. Anselm dialogues about the number of angels who rebelled against God and whether the same number of humans will replace them. While this discussion of angels seems speculative, it is not completely void of relevance. In this dialogue, Anselm raises crucial issues regarding the justice of God, the fallenness of humans and some angels (including Satan), God's willing redemption of humanity, and the inability of humanity to pay the debt owed to God.

This digression compels the reader to see that God justly rules the whole cosmos and that every rational creature (including angels) is subject to God's will. This idea has particular significance for cultural contexts that often dismiss the supernatural and God's sovereignty, and tend to be very human-centered. We must, however, be careful about the undiscerning appropriation of his theological ideas. For instance, employing Anselm's "numerically perfect reasoning" method without concern for its biblical merit could lead to seeing false significance in numbers.

As J. I. Packer rightly points out, doctrinal knowledge and practical significance should go hand in hand, particularly when it comes to spiritual flourishing.

> To be preoccupied with getting theological knowledge as an end in itself . . . with no higher motive than a desire to know all the answers, is the direct route to a state of self-satisfied self-deception. We need to guard our hearts against such an attitude, and pray to be kept from it . . . There can be no spiritual health without doctrinal knowledge; but it is equally true that there can be no spiritual health *with* it, if it is sought for the wrong purpose and valued by the wrong standard. In this way, doctrinal study really can become a danger to spiritual life, and we today, no less than the Corinthians of old, need to be on guard here.[9]

When Jesus called his followers to be his disciples, he wanted them to know him not only intellectually, but also to follow him in every area of life. He proclaimed, "If anyone would come after me, let him deny himself and take up his cross

---

9. J. I. Packer, *Knowing God* (Downers Grove, IL: InterVarsity, 2018), 22, italics original.

and follow me" (Matthew 16:24). Theology ultimately should compel us to do just that: follow Christ. As John Webster explains, truly "theological theology" joyfully testifies to the truth of the gospel—"the norm of the Church's praise, confession, and action . . . and of its understanding of nature and human reality."[10]

PUTTING IT ALL TOGETHER: AN EXAMPLE OF EVALUATING AND APPLYING THEOLOGY

In the winter term of 1899-1900, Adolf von Harnack delivered an important lecture series at the University of Berlin to answer the question, "What is Christianity?" Scholars had previously sought the answer to this question in the Bible or in their church's creeds. For von Harnack, however, the historical-critical method was the most reliable theological approach, and its results were both true and reliable.

In these lectures, the German scholar, who was the son of Lutheran scholar Theodosius Harnack, sought to strip away the "husk" of the culturally bound teachings of Christ and the church in order to discover the "kernel," or eternal truths, of the Christian faith. Von Harnack consciously rejected the Christianity of the creeds and confessions and even the Gospels, asserting that Christian dogma (articles of faith) and Scripture have been influenced by their cultures and by Greek philosophy. Von Harnack presupposed an anti-supernatural, anthropocentric (human-centered) worldview, arguing that the essence of Christianity is the fatherhood of God, the brotherhood of humanity, the infinite value of the human soul, and the call to higher righteousness.

10. John Webster, "Discovering Dogmatics," in *Shaping a Theological Mind: Theological Context and Methodology*, ed. Darren C. Marks (Burlington, VT: Ashgate, 2002), 135.

Jesus, according to von Harnack, was not divine, but a historical man who had a unique consciousness of God as the Father and his Father. The heart of Christ's teachings, the "Gospel . . . has to do with the Father only and not with the Son."[11] It points to the "value of all mankind," which is to be lived out in love of God and love of neighbor.[12] Christianity is essentially a practical matter of knowing God as Father rather than believing in historically bound Christian dogma such as the Trinity and the two natures of Christ.

After carefully reading von Harnack and understanding his historical and cultural context, the theological genre, and his views, one is prepared to begin assessing the work. His perspective has vast implications for our views of revelation, God, anthropology, Christology, soteriology, eschatology, and the Christian life. It establishes reason and the historical method as authoritative rather than Scripture. God is simply our loving Father, not also our divine Judge; humanity is good, not fallen and in need of salvation; Christ was a historical man, not our divine Savior; humans save themselves, not Christ; the kingdom of God is a present reality within ourselves, not to be completed in the future; and the ethics of love are the gospel, not an outgrowth of it.

Some of these implications appeal strongly to our current culture, which has witnessed great evil and suffering and seeks to understand God as a loving Father who values all humans. Furthermore, this work exemplifies how culture has a shaping influence on Christianity and stresses the importance of living out one's faith. If von Harnack's views are adopted without discernment, however, one will ultimately be left with an anthropocentric (human-centered) theology that

---

11. Adolf von Harnack, *What Is Christianity?* rev. ed., trans. Thomas Bailey Sanders (New York: Putnam, 1908), 154.

12. Von Harnack, *What Is Christianity?* 73, 79.

leaves no room for the cross, the resurrection, and ultimately salvation.

In *What Is Christianity?* von Harnack promotes confidence in reason and a bottom-up theology that emphasizes human-kind and the kingdom of God being fulfilled here on earth and establishes Jesus as merely a teacher of timeless morality and self-esteem. Therefore, true faith at best is limited to doing what Jesus did. Von Harnack's liberal theology and antipathy toward dogma ultimately led him and other scholars away from the Lutheran church to embracing German national-ism instead.

Von Harnack's theology serves as a cautionary tale of what can happen when we prioritize our thoughts and scholarly methodologies over the truthfulness of God's Word. He also helps us think through the important issues such as the role of the church in determining dogma and what are the essentials and nonessentials of the faith. Reading von Harnack has value in helping the reader think through many topics, including the significance of the context of doctrine, church authority, who is Christ, and what are the essentials of the gospel.

CONCLUSION

Mortimer Adler argues that "a good book can teach you about the world and about yourself." By engaging with good books, you become not only more knowledgeable but also wiser as you become "more deeply aware of the great and enduring truths [or, for that matter, the great fallacies] of human life."[13] Sometimes this can even happen by dialoguing with an author with whom you find yourself in disagreement. But the real purpose of theology is not just understanding ourselves or the

---

13. Mortimer J. Adler and Charles Van Doren, *How to Read a Book* (New York: Simon & Schuster, 1972), 340–41.

world, or even learning to value other perspectives. It is to truly know and worship the living God. Factual, conceptual, critical, and practical inquiries are important to understanding both *what* is being communicated in a theological work and *how* the ideas should be evaluated and applied.

As René Descartes aptly stated, "The reading of all good books is like a conversation with the most honorable people of past ages." He continued: "Theology teaches one how to reach heaven."[14] A theological conversation between the author and reader ultimately becomes valuable when the reader moves beyond merely reading the words on the page, or even understanding the meaning of the author, and is brought closer to God. As Descartes pointed out, this step is only possible if one is able to know the "true worth" of the author's words so as "to guard against being deceived."

Once one has been trained in *how* to listen to the author—discerning the context, the theological genre, and the author's view—one can move from merely asking questions of the text to giving an informed and appreciative response. This process should include prayerful and biblical evaluation of the text and seeing its possible application in one's own life. In all the theological works we read, our goal should be the transformation of our hearts and minds to conform to Christ. Romans 12:2 encourages just that: "Do not be conformed to this world but be transformed by the renewal of your mind, that by testing you may discern what is the will of God, what is good and acceptable and perfect."

---

14. René Descartes, *Philosophical Essays and Correspondence*, ed. Roger Ariew (Indianapolis, IN: Hackett, 2000), 48.

QUESTIONS FOR DISCUSSION AND REFLECTION

1. Kevin Vanhoozer writes, "Doctrine forms disciples when it helps the church to act out its new life in Christ." Give an example of a doctrine that has helped you act out your new life in Christ.

2. If you were reading a book review of a theological work, how would you know if the reviewer was a good critic of the work? How can this inform the way you evaluate theological works?

3. What are a few differences between the way you approach a theological text in your initial reading and in your reappraisal of it?

4. Why is it important to discern the coherence of a work? How should you view a work that lacks coherence?

5. Biblical veracity should be the primary criteria for evaluating a theological work. Examine George Herbert's poem "Love (III)," printed in this chapter, looking for at least one example of a biblical truth.

6. It is important to assess the significance of a theological work, seeking to discover its practical and spiritual value. Name one insight from this chapter that you can employ in your reading that will help in this process.

7. Theology is to be lived. In reading theology, it is vital to ask the question, *So what?* What is the most pressing question you have that you would like theology to speak into?

8. In the "Putting It All Together" section, we discussed Adolf von Harnack's view of Christ and the gospel. What is one valuable thing you can learn from dialoguing with von Harnack, even if you disagree with him? Would you encourage someone to read *What Is Christianity?* Explain your answer.

9. Romans 12:2 encourages us, "Do not be conformed to this world but be transformed by the renewal of your mind, that by testing you may discern what is the will of God, what is good and acceptable and perfect." Name one way you can seek to transform your mind today.

PRACTICE EVALUATING AND APPLYING THE THEOLOGICAL TEXT

What is the value of the work?

Continue to pray for discernment and briefly reassess a theological work you have read and answer the following questions:

1. What does careful inspection of the theological text reveal about the work?
2. What is the coherency, veracity, and significance of the text?
   - How coherent is the theological text?
   - How truthful is the work?
   - What is the significance of the theological ideas/principles in the text?
3. What are the practical implications and possible applications of this work for the individual, the church, and society?
4. What is the value of the work?

Equipping Others to Read Theology for All Its Worth

And if the student finds that this is not to his taste? Well, that is regrettable. Most regrettable. His taste should not be consulted; it is being formed.

FLANNERY O'CONNOR,
MYSTERY AND MANNERS

Iron sharpens iron,
    and one man sharpens another.
PROVERBS 27:17

How can we equip others to read theology?

Charles Spurgeon recalls an American military tale of a man passing a group of soldiers hard at work lifting a heavy piece of timber. The corporal of the regiment was calling out orders and directions to his soldiers. The passerby dismounted his horse and asked the corporal, "What is the good of your calling out to those men, why don't you help them yourself and do part of the work?" The corporal responded indignantly, "Perhaps you are not aware to whom you are speaking, sir; I am a corporal." "I beg your pardon," replied the onlooker; "you are a corporal are you; I am sorry I should have insulted you." The man then took off his coat and helped the soldiers build the fortification. Upon finishing he said, "Mr. Corporal, I am sorry I insulted you, but when you have any more fortifications to get up, and your men won't help you, send for George Washington, the commander-in-chief, and I will come and help them." Feeling ashamed of himself, the corporal slunk away.[1]

Similarly, Christ, our commander-in-chief, gives us an example of how to lead those entrusted to us. He did not lead his disciples by standing apart from them and shouting out commands. Rather, the Gospels reveal Jesus walking alongside them, teaching and modeling godly living. Jesus Christ did not just convey head knowledge, but he equipped his disciples with the tools to live lives that glorify God. Christ trained them to know God and to recognize their utter dependence on him (John 15:15). Christ invited them to listen to God, seek God's ways, and put off the ways of this world (Matthew 6:33). He called his followers to seek godly wisdom (John 17:17).

---

1. Charles Haddon Spurgeon, "A Home Mission Sermon," no. 259, June 26, 1859, Spurgeon Center for Biblical Preaching, www.spurgeon.org/resource -library/sermons/a-home-mission-sermon.

In a similar vein, we too need to humbly walk beside others, helping them to fulfill their Christian call to love the Lord God with all their heart and to love their neighbors as themselves (Matthew 22:37). How do we pursue this calling in a theological learning context? The role of a Christian educator, as Helmut Thielicke points out in his classic text *A Little Exercise for Young Theologians,* is to see and listen to students "not only as students but also as souls entrusted" to us.[2] How do we help others discern godly wisdom? That is one of the primary tasks of the Christian educator, mentor, or fellow Christian. Higher learning, in general, requires that one go beyond merely understanding words printed on the page in the pursuit of knowledge. For the Christian, the goal of studying theology is not just knowledge but godly wisdom, with the ultimate end of hearing and responding to God's Word. Reading theological works should serve that end.

As Socrates rightly noted, "The unexamined life is not worth living." He offered questioning and reasoning as the sources of human significance. We can agree in part with Socrates that we are called to examine life and to seek wisdom. However, as C. S. Lewis pointed out in *The Abolition of Man,* mere humanistic rationalism leads to secularism. Endless questioning and reasoning do not result in real knowledge and godliness, but ultimately lead to meaninglessness.[3] Lewis also warns against trivializing emotions: "For every one pupil who needs to be guarded from a weak excess of sensibility there are three who need to be awakened from the slumber of cold vulgarity. The task of the modern educator is not to cut down jungles but to irrigate deserts. The right defence against false sentiments is to inculcate just sentiments."[4]

---

2. Helmut Thielicke, *A Little Exercise for Young Theologians* (Grand Rapids: Eerdmans, 2016), 16.

3. See C. S. Lewis, *The Abolition of Man* (1944; repr., New York: HarperOne, 2001), 80–81.

4. Lewis, *Abolition of Man,* 13–14.

As Lewis infers, Christian education should differ from Socrates's rationalistic approach by maintaining a God-centered perspective that informs both the mind and the heart. It should lead us to acknowledge that we are perpetual disciples of Christ. As Christians, we ought to guide others to dialogue with the Lord and with each other for the purpose of growing in knowledge and wisdom and serving Christ with our whole selves (Mark 12:28–30).

An excellent theological education should not teach one to see Scripture as merely a repository of propositions to be mastered or stories to interpret as they see fit. God's Word is given to us for the purpose of drawing us into a relationship with our neighbor and our Creator, Sustainer, Redeemer, and Sanctifier. Unlike other disciplines, theological education gives us the opportunity to inquire into not only what God *has* said, but also what God *is* saying and how we should think about and respond to it. Theological texts can help us do just that.

In 1963, American Catholic novelist Flannery O'Connor cautioned literature teachers about allowing student preferences to guide their pedagogical choices. She asserts that a student's "taste should not be consulted; it is being formed." Teachers only fulfill their responsibility when they "guide" their students through the "best writing," shaping their tastes. She urged teachers to return to "their proper business of preparing foundations."[5] Scripture calls us to this very task, preparing foundations by training *minds* and *hearts*. This training will enable the reader to discern God's truth—the truth about themselves, God, and their relationship to him—wherever it is spoken, and seek to correctly apply it to their daily lives (Romans 8:14; 12:2; Ephesians 4:23; Colossians 3:10).

Often we forget the importance of training one how to

---

5. Flannery O'Connor, *Mystery and Manners: Occasional Prose*, ed. Sally and Robert Fitzgerald (New York: Farrar, Straus & Giroux, 1969), 140.

listen and ask the question, "What do you think?" prior to "What does the author think?" This approach can lead students to give uninformed opinions or even reject the value of a work before having truly understood it. Furthermore, the reader can come away seeing the text as merely a mirror of their own thoughts rather than as a window into other perspectives on a topic and an opportunity to train their hearts and minds to love what is good (Romans 12:9).

If we coach others to listen to the text as they would listen to a dear friend, they will be more open to appreciating the merit of the work, even if they find themselves in disagreement with it. They should not be led to believe that the value of a theological work is based on uninformed personal preference, but rather on how it can move them toward understanding and properly loving God and loving others. Sometimes this happens when a theological work helps point out flaws in their thinking or makes them aware of the dangers of holding to an idea.

We can provide a type of "scaffolding" to guide others in *how* to listen well to theological texts. Russian cultural-historical psychologist Lev Vygotsky suggested that one can aid in the learning process by providing scaffolding, or assistance, until the learner can accomplish the task alone.[6] It is not enough to give them the information they need to understand and respond to theological texts, yelling orders to them like the corporal in the story. Instead, like George Washington, we should come alongside other theological readers and assist them in learning *how* to approach theological writings.

A practical way to equip them is to encourage them to be good conversation partners with theological works by prayerfully asking the right kinds of questions and then pursuing the answers. These questions can be placed in the following

---

6. See Christine Sarikas, "Vygotsky Scaffolding: What It Is and How to Use It," PrepScholar, July 10, 2018, https://blog.prepscholar.com/vygotsky-scaffolding-zone-of-proximal-development.

categories: discerning the context, the theological framework, sources, and the theologian's view. These questions include factual, interpretive, and assessment questions.

Once the readers have the tools of careful inspection, they will be better equipped to dialogue with theological works on their own and discern the theological truths communicated in them. They can practice reading theology for all its worth by "dialoguing" the theological works they read and engaging in "theological discussions." Each of these activities will be discussed below.

TEACHING HOW TO DIALOGUE A THEOLOGICAL WORK

We all have experienced spending hours of concerted effort to master a skill. Recent research has debunked the idea that "practice makes perfect," noting that other important factors such as natural ability, how early in life you were introduced to an activity, and intrinsic motivation also contribute to success. That does not indicate, however, that practice is not important.

Certainly, some readers are naturally more adept than others at understanding and assessing theological texts. Even these people, however, will benefit from training in the art of reading theology and from the opportunity to practice productively dialoguing with a text. Just as we wouldn't expect an elite athlete to successfully compete at a high level without coaching and regular training, we shouldn't expect someone to read a theological text with competence without some guidance and practice. Regular practice of the tools of careful inspection described in this book is vital to improving comprehension and analysis.

One way to facilitate practice is to assign them to read and "dialogue" primary source theological works. Too often we rely on secondary sources or lectures to explain the teachings of various theologians, thereby rendering the learner dependent on others to discern the value of a theological work. Instead, we should encourage others to return to the original sources (*ad fontes*), particularly the Bible and theological texts, to learn directly from "so great a cloud of witnesses" (Hebrews 12:1), just as the Reformers did in the sixteenth century.

A list of important theological works is supplied in appendix 2 to assist you in choosing texts. To help others practice reading these texts well, they may "dialogue" the texts. This is not, however, a traditional thesis-based outline, but rather a condensed set of answers to the questions discussed in this book. Dialoguing with the work by writing out answers to the questions will help them consider the context, the framework, the sources, and the author's viewpoint, and then assess and apply the work.

Just as parents can aid their child in learning to walk by supporting them and gradually giving less aid as the child grows more capable of walking alone, you can assist others in developing their capacity to effectively read theological texts. Initially, you should walk them through the "dialogue" before the first reading, assisting them in finding the answers. Then ask them to complete the process on their own, giving them hints beforehand regarding how to answer the questions, and ample feedback afterward so they understand how to improve in their reading of the text. Meaningful feedback can aid in the development of their reading comprehension, critical thinking skills, and ability to discover possible practical applications of the text. As they progress in their reading, they should need less assistance and should begin to read with the aforementioned questions in mind.

Appendix 3 can serve as a guide for written theological dialogues. You can further tailor it to your needs. You may find that some have a harder time with identifying the method and presuppositions, and you may choose to cover these in a talk or assist them in the process of discerning them. Ultimately the goal of these written dialogues is to help theological readers practice the tools of careful inspection in order to improve their understanding of the theological text and listen more effectively. This appendix should also enhance theological discussions. If every participant enters into a discussion having already addressed these questions, the discussion can move beyond recall or comprehension to understanding and assessing the text on a deeper level.

FACILITATING THEOLOGICAL DISCUSSIONS

If theology is to be more than a discipline for the academically elite, we need to equip others to engage in rich theological conversations that lead to Christian knowledge and growth. Discussion-based learning gives readers an opportunity to challenge one another to dig deep into theological texts, cultivate critical thinking skills, and develop a learned sensitivity to the perspectives of others. Theological discussions should go beyond mere factual and conceptual inquiries, which primarily focus on recall and comprehension. While these tasks are not unimportant, meaningful discussion should facilitate growth by including critical and practical inquiries that explore the ideas of the text in order to evaluate and consider their practical application.

A theological discussion can help us think analytically, express ideas effectively, and listen attentively to a theological text in a community setting. Theological works are important because they force us to think about meaningful questions: Who is God? Who are we? What can we know? How should we act? What can we hope for? The better we understand the answers, the more equipped we are to know God, ourselves, and the world around us, and how we should live our lives in submission to Christ.

The role of the leader is to ask questions that help the group explore the ideas in the work. The participants may also ask questions and offer answers. All responses should be based on the reading of the text; it is usually best to avoid references to outside sources (except other works already discussed and the Bible). The leader should encourage participants to agree or disagree with what the author and other participants say and ask them to back up their perspectives with reasons based on the text and Scripture.

There are three main types of questions that a discussion leader can ask about a theological work:

1. **Factual Questions:** Factual questions have one correct answer. These include questions regarding definitions, the background of the work and author, or details of the text. They require the participant to offer quotations or paraphrases of the work.
   - *Example:* What analogies does Cyprian use in *On the Unity of the Church* to demonstrate the church's unity while being dispersed throughout the world?
2. **Interpretative Questions:** Interpretative questions explore what the author means by what he or she says. They are open-ended questions that lead to an extended discussion of ideas in the text and can elicit multiple responses.
   - *Example:* What is the primary reason Cyprian is arguing that church unity is essential? In other words, is it an issue of correct theology, right polity, a defense against heresy, related to salvation, or another reason?
3. **Assessment Questions:** Assessment questions, which include evaluative and application questions, require the reader to appraise the veracity and value of the work and the extent to which the work has application to their own life, the church, and the world.
   - *Example:* How well does Cyprian's stance on church unity accord with Psalm 133; John 17:20–23; 1 Corinthians 1:10–17; and Ephesians 4:1–16? What should be the basis of church unity?

Whenever possible, formulate open-ended questions that guide the group to discover for themselves the answers in the text. To keep a discussion focused on listening to the work, a theological discussion should employ questions that help the group comprehend the text before moving on to assessing it. It is profitable to open a theological conversation with a "basic question" that explores a key idea or theme of the work, which can lead to an extended discussion. A strong basic question is open-ended and interpretative and can generate different responses that help clarify and develop the most important ideas of the work.

The follow-up questions contain ideas that are subordinate but related to the basic question. They can include questions of fact and interpretation. Their primary function is to help the group resolve the basic question by encouraging participants to further develop their ideas, clarify their understanding of the text, and consider other possible responses.

It is important to avoid asking assessment questions prior to asking the basic question and the follow-ups. Questions of evaluation and application are most meaningful after the group has thoroughly discussed questions related to the interpretation of the text. Assessment questions may get a discussion started, but they can quickly turn it into a polling of likes and dislikes or a defense of premature judgments. Instead, assessment questions should concern themselves with the truth or the fitting application of theological ideas from the work.

Appendixes 4 and 5 contain helpful guides for participating in and leading a discussion. These guides are modeled in part after the "Shared Inquiry" approach that has been used in Great Books programs. To challenge others to get the most out of a theological discussion, they may be trained in how to lead a conversation themselves. By writing their own discussion questions, they will be encouraged to apprehend the text and cultivate theological discussions that guide others to pursue knowledge and godly wisdom. You can begin by modeling for them how to facilitate a discussion and then allowing them to lead one of their own. Appendix 5 can serve as a guide for formulating discussion questions.

CONCLUSION

It is important for theological facilitators to help train others' heads, hearts, and hands to think about, love, and do what is good, pure, and true. Theological books can serve as great partners in this pursuit if they are read with a learned discernment. In *The Prophetic Imagination*, Walter Brueggemann provides a vision for the ministry of a theological educator:

> I suggest that the dominant culture, now and in every time, is grossly uncritical, cannot tolerate serious and fundamental criticism, and will go to great lengths to stop it. Conversely, the dominant culture is a wearied culture, nearly unable to be seriously energized to new promises from God . . . And we may even suggest that to choose between criticizing and energizing is the temptation, respectively, of liberalism and conservatism. Liberals are good at criticism but often have no word of promise to speak; conservatives tend to future well and invite to alternative visions, but a germane criticism by the prophet is often not forthcoming. For those of us personally charged with this ministry, we may observe that to be called where this dialectic is maintained is an awesome call. And each of us is likely to fall to one side or the other.[7]

Brueggemann's words speak as much into our situation as they did when they were first published in 1978. Christians

---

7. Walter Brueggemann, *The Prophetic Imagination*, 40th anniv. ed. (Minneapolis: Fortress, 2018), 4–5.

often struggle to engage in productive critical reflection and to find life-giving biblical hope in Christ. Brueggemann suggests that the task of prophetic ministry, as exemplified in the Old Testament prophets, is to "nurture, nourish, and evoke a consciousness and perception alternative to the consciousness and perception of the dominant culture around us."[8] The prophet accomplishes this work in the context of a community by understanding the dominant culture and energizing the community toward a vision that is grounded in God's plan. Brueggemann reminds us that real criticism starts in the capacity to grieve, acknowledging that things are not the way they are supposed to be. Yet the true prophet not only critiques but also seeks to energize the community from apathy to an alternate mode of life.

Christians are called to such a prophetic ministry. We are to "nurture, nourish, and evoke" in others a radically different consciousness—one that is captive to the Word of God, not simply to the world (2 Corinthians 1:12), one that is not susceptible to every cultural whim but is concerned with guarding and proclaiming "the good deposit entrusted to you" (2 Timothy 1:14). We can assist others in this pursuit by equipping them with the tools to read and discuss theology with discernment. With the proper tools, readers will be able to approach theological texts with confidence and intentionality, learning to identify worthy dialogue partners who can assist them in knowing and loving God and others and living lives worthy of their calling in Christ.

---

8. Brueggemann, *Prophetic Imagination*, 3.

A Selected List of Significant Theologians and Theological Works

THEOLOGICAL WORKS

Apostles' Creed
Clement of Rome (ca. 30–100)
   First Epistle of Clement to the Corinthians
Ignatius of Antioch (ca. 35–110)
   The Epistle of Ignatius to the Ephesians
Polycarp (ca. 80–155)
   The Epistle of Polycarp to the Philippians
Justin Martyr (ca. 100–165)
   The First Apology of Justin
   The Second Apology of Justin
Irenaeus of Lyons (ca. 130–202)
   Against the Heresies
Clement of Alexandria (ca. 150–211/216)
   Trilogy: *Protrepticus, Paedagogus,* and *Stromata*
Tertullian (ca. 160–220)
   Apology
Origen of Alexandria (ca. 184–254)
   Hexapla
   On First Principles

John Chrysostom (ca. 347–407)
  Homilies of John Chrysostom
Cyprian (ca. 200–258)
  The Unity of the Church
Athanasius of Alexandria (298–373)
  On the Incarnation
Nicene Creed (325)
Gregory of Nazianzus (347–407)
  On God and Christ
Jerome (ca. 347–420)
  The Latin Vulgate
Saint Augustine of Hippo (354–430)
  On the Trinity
  On Christian Doctrine
  The City of God
Cyril of Alexandria (ca. 378–444)
  On the Unity of Christ
  Second and Third Letters to Nestorius and John of Antioch
Nicene-Constantinopolitan Creed (381)
Leo's Tome (449)
Definition of Chalcedon (451)
Saint Benedict (ca. 480–547)
  The Rule
Gregory the Great (540–604)
  On Pastoral Care
Anselm of Canterbury (1033–1109)
  Why God Became Man
Peter Abelard (1079–1142)
  Sic et Non
Bernard of Clairvaux (1090–1153)
  On Loving God
  Sermons on the Song of Songs
Peter Lombard (1096–1160)
  Sentences

Francis of Assisi (1182–1226)
Little Flowers of St. Francis
Bonaventure (1221–1274)
The Soul's Journey into God
Thomas Aquinas (1225–1274)
Summa Theologica
Summa Contra Gentiles
William of Ockham (1285–1347)
Opera philosophica et theologica
Julian of Norwich (ca. 1342–1416)
Revelations of Divine Love
Catherine of Siena (1347–1380)
The Dialogue of St. Catherine of Siena
Thomas à Kempis (1380–1471)
The Imitation of Christ
Desiderius Erasmus (1469–1536)
In Praise of Folly
On the Freedom of the Will
Martin Luther (1483–1546)
95 Theses
Freedom of the Christian
Bondage of the Will
The Heidelberg Disputation
Ulrich Zwingli (1484–1531)
67 Articles
Commentary on True and False Religion
Thomas Cranmer (1489–1556)
Book of Common Prayer
Homilies
Thirty-nine Articles (1571)
Ignatius of Loyola (1491–1556)
Letters and Instructions
Menno Simons (1496–1561)
The Spiritual Resurrection

Foundation of Christian Doctrine
Philipp Melanchthon (1497–1560)
  Augsburg Confession
John Calvin (1509–1564)
  Institutes of the Christian Religion
  Commentaries
John Knox (1514–1572)
  *The First Blast of the Trumpet against the Monstrous
    Regiment of Women*
  Appellations to the Nobility and Commonality of Scotland
  Confession of Faith, the *First Book of Discipline*, and *The
    Book of Common Order*
Teresa of Avila (1515–1582)
  Way of Perfection
  Interior Castle
Theodore Beza (1519–1605)
  On the Rights of the Magistrate
  Tractationes theologicae
  Summa totius Christianismi
Schleitheim Confession (1527)
Canons and Decrees of the Council of Trent (1545–1563)
Richard Hooker (1554–1600)
  Of the Laws of Ecclesiastical Polity
William Perkins (1558–1602)
  A Golden Chain
Jacobus Arminius (1560–1609)
  *On the Righteousness and Efficacy of the Providence of God
    Concerning Evil*
  Declaration of Sentiments
Heidelberg Catechism (1563)
Five Articles of Remonstrance (1610)
Richard Baxter (1615–1691)
  Reformed Liturgy
  Reformed Pastor

Canons of the Synod of Dort (1618–1619)
John Owen (1618–1683)
  The Mortification of Sin
  The Priesthood of Christ
Francis Turretin (1623–1687)
  Institutes of Elenctic Theology
John Bunyan (1628–1688)
  The Pilgrim's Progress
Westminster Confession (1646)
Jonathan Edwards (1703–1758)
  Religious Affections
  The End for Which God Created the World
  Freedom of the Will
  On Original Sin
John Wesley (1703–1791)
  A Plain Account of Christian Perfection
George Whitefield (1714–1770)
  Sermons by George Whitefield
John Newton (1725–1807)
  Thoughts Upon the African Slave Trade
Friedrich Schleiermacher (1768–1834)
  On Religion
  The Christian Faith
Charles Hodge (1797–1878)
  Systematic Theology
John Henry Newman (1801–1890)
  Essay on the Development of Christian Doctrine
  The Idea of a University
Horace Bushnell (1802–1876)
  Discourses on Christian Nurture
  God in Christ
  Nature and the Supernatural
Søren Kierkegaard (1813–1855)
  Either/Or

Fear and Trembling
Albert Ritschl (1822–1889)
   The Christian Doctrine of Justification and Reconciliation
Abraham Kuyper (1837–1920)
   Common Grace
   Pro Rege
B. B. Warfield (1851–1921)
   The Lord of Glory
   The Inspiration and Authority of the Bible
   The Person and Work of Christ
Adolf von Harnack (1851–1930)
   History of Dogma
   What Is Christianity?
Walter Rauschenbusch (1861–1918)
   Christianizing the Social Order
   A Theology for the Social Gospel
   The Social Principles of Jesus
Vatican I (1868–1870)
Lewis Sperry Chafer (1871–1952)
   Systematic Theology
Louis Berkhof (1873–1957)
   Systematic Theology
J. Gresham Machen (1881–1937)
   The Origin of Paul's Religion
   Christianity and Liberalism
Rudolf Bultmann (1884–1976)
   Faith and Understanding
   New Testament and Mythology
   Kerygma and Myth
Paul Tillich (1886–1965)
   Systematic Theology
   Dynamics of Faith
Karl Barth (1886–1968)
   The Epistle to the Romans

    Evangelical Theology
    Church Dogmatics
Reinhold Niebuhr (1892–1971)
    The Nature and Destiny of Man
Karl Rahner (1904–1984)
    Foundations of Christian Faith
    The Trinity
Hans Urs von Balthasar (1905–1988)
    The Glory of the Lord
    A Theology of History
Dietrich Bonhoeffer (1906–1945)
    The Cost of Discipleship
    Life Together
Francis Schaeffer (1912–1984)
    Trilogy: *The God Who Is There, Escape from Reason,*
       and *He Is There and He Is Not Silent*
Carl F. H. Henry (1913–2003)
    God, Revelation, and Authority
Edward Schillebeeckx (1914–2009)
    Jesus: An Experiment in Christology
    Church: The Human Story of God
Avery Dulles (1918–2008)
    Church and Society
    Models of the Church
Langdon Gilkey (1919–2004)
    Message and Existence: An Introduction to Christian
       Theology
John Hick (1922–2012)
    A Christian Theology of Religions
    God Has Many Names
    The Metaphor of God Incarnate
John B. Cobb Jr. (b. 1925)
    Process Theology
    Toward a Universal Theology of Religion

Jürgen Moltmann (b. 1926)

> Trilogy of Theological Works: *Theology of Hope, The Crucified God*, and *The Church in the Power of the Spirit*
>
> *God in Creation: An Ecological Doctrine of Creation*

Gustavo Gutiérrez (b. 1928)

> *A Theology of Liberation: History, Politics, and Salvation*

Hans Küng (b. 1928)

> *Infallible? An Inquiry*
>
> *Theology for the Third Millennium: An Ecumenical View*
>
> *Eternal Life? Life after Death as a Medical, Philosophical, and Theological Problem*

Mary Daly (1928–2010)

> *Beyond God the Father: Toward a Philosophy of Women's Liberation*

Wolfhart Pannenberg (1928–2014)

> *Systematic Theology*

Walter Brueggemann (b. 1933)

> *An Unsettling God: The Heart of the Hebrew Bible*

Sallie McFague (1933–2019)

> *Metaphorical Theology: Models of God in Religious Language*
>
> *Models of God: Theology for an Ecological, Nuclear Age*

James Cone (1936–2018)

> *A Black Theology of Liberation*
>
> *The Cross and the Lynching Tree*

David Tracy (b. 1939)

> *The Analogical Imagination*

Stanley Hauerwas (b. 1940)

> *The Peaceable Kingdom: A Primer in Christian Ethics*
>
> *Resident Aliens: Life in the Christian Colony*

Elizabeth A. Johnson (b. 1941)

> *She Who Is: The Mystery of God in Feminist Theological Discourse*

Ellen T. Charry (b. 1947)

> "For God's Sake: The Wall of Hostility Has Come Down"

God and the Art of Happiness

N. T. Wright (b. 1948)

The Resurrection of the Son of God

Wayne Grudem (b. 1948)

Systematic Theology: An Introduction to Biblical Doctrine

Stanley Grenz (1950–2005)

Theology for the Community of God

Miroslav Volf (b. 1956)

Allah: A Christian Response

After Our Likeness: The Church as the Image of the Trinity

Exclusion and Embrace: A Theological Exploration of Identity, Otherness, and Reconciliation

Greg Boyd (b. 1957)

God of the Possible: A Biblical Introduction to the Open View of God

Kevin J. Vanhoozer (b. 1957)

Is There a Meaning in This Text? The Bible, the Reader, and the Morality of Literary Knowledge

The Drama of Doctrine: A Canonical-Linguistic Approach to Christian Theology

Veli-Matti Kärkkäinen (b. 1958)

Constructive Christian Theology for the Church in the Pluralistic World

Michael Scott Horton (b. 1964)

The Christian Faith: A Systematic Theology for Pilgrims on the Way

Vatican II (1962–1965)

DICTIONARIES OF THEOLOGY

Alexander, T. Desmond, Brian S. Rosner, D. A. Carson, and Graeme Goldsworthy, eds. *New Dictionary of Biblical Theology: Exploring the Unity and Diversity of Scripture.* Downers Grove, IL: InterVarsity, 2000.

Elwell, Walter A., ed. *Evangelical Dictionary of Biblical Theology*. Grand Rapids: Baker, 1996.

Erickson, Millard, J., ed. *The Concise Dictionary of Christian Theology*. Rev. ed. Wheaton, IL: Crossway, 2001.

Ferguson, Sinclair B., J. I. Packer, and David F. Wright, eds. *New Dictionary of Theology*. 3rd ed. Downers Grove, IL: InterVarsity Press, 1988.

Hastings, Adrian, Alistair Mason, and Hugh Pyper, eds. *The Oxford Companion to Christian Thought*. New York: Oxford University Press, 2000.

Hays, J. Daniel, J. Scott Duvall, and C. Marvin Pate, eds. *Dictionary of Biblical Prophecy and End Times*. Grand Rapids: Zondervan, 2007.

Holloman, Henry W., ed. *Kregel Dictionary of the Bible and Theology*. Grand Rapids: Kregel, 2005.

McKim, Donald K., ed. *Westminster Dictionary of Theological Terms*. Louisville, KY: Westminster John Knox, 1996.

Richardson, Alan, and John Bowden, eds. *The Westminster Dictionary of Christian Theology*. Louisville, KY: Westminster John Knox, 1983.

Treier, Daniel J., and Walter A. Elwell, eds. *Evangelical Dictionary of Theology*. 3rd ed. Grand Rapids: Baker, 2017.

ANTHOLOGIES OF THEOLOGY

Bettenson, Henry, and Chris Maunder, eds. *Documents of the Christian Church*. 4th ed. New York: Oxford University Press, 2011.

Janz, Denis R. *A Reformation Reader*. 2nd ed. Minneapolis, MN: Fortress Press, 2008.

McGrath, Alister E. *The Christian Theology Reader*. 5th ed. Oxford: Blackwell, 2017.

———. *Theology: The Basic Readings*. 3rd ed. Oxford: Blackwell, 2018.

Placher, William C. *Readings in the History of Christian Theology*. 2 vols. Philadelphia: Westminster, 1988.

HISTORICAL THEOLOGY RESOURCES

Benedetto, Robert, ed. *The New Westminster Dictionary of Church History*. 2nd ed. 2 vols. Louisville, KY: Westminster John Knox, 2008–.

Bercot, David W., ed. *A Dictionary of Early Christian Beliefs*. Peabody, MA: Hendrickson, 1998.

Cross, F. L., and E. A. Livingstone, eds. *Oxford Dictionary of the Christian Church*. 3rd rev. ed. New York: Oxford University Press, 2005.

Douglas, J. D., ed. *The New International Dictionary of the Christian Church*. Rev. ed. Grand Rapids: Zondervan, 1993.

González, Justo L., ed. *The Westminster Dictionary of Theologians*. Louisville, KY: Westminster John Knox, 2006.

Hart, Trevor A., ed. *The Dictionary of Historical Theology*. Grand Rapids: Eerdmans, 2000.

Larsen, Timothy T., David W. Bebbington, and Mark A. Noll, eds. *Biographical Dictionary of Evangelicals*. Downers Grove, IL: InterVarsity, 2003.

McKim, Donald K., ed. *Dictionary of Major Biblical Interpreters*. Downers Grove, IL: InterVarsity, 2007.

HISTORICAL THEOLOGY TEXTBOOKS

Ahlstrom, Sydney E. *A Religious History of the American People*. 2nd ed. New Haven, CT: Yale University Press, 2004.

Allison, Gregg R. *Historical Theology: An Introduction to Christian Doctrine*. Grand Rapids: Zondervan, 2011.

Ferguson, Everett. *From Christ to Pre-Reformation: The Rise and Growth of the Church in Its Cultural, Intellectual, and*

Political Context. Vol. 1 of *Church History.* Grand Rapids: Zondervan, 2005.

Hastings, Adrian. *A World History of Christianity.* Grand Rapids: Eerdmans, 2000.

Lindberg, Carter, ed. *The Reformation Theologians: An Introduction to Theology in the Early Modern Period.* Malden, MA: Blackwell, 2002.

McGrath, Alister E. *Historical Theology: An Introduction to the History of Christian Thought.* 2nd ed. Malden, MA: Wiley-Blackwell, 2013.

Muller, Richard A. *Post-Reformation Reformed Dogmatics: The Rise and Development of Reformed Orthodoxy.* Grand Rapids: Baker, 2003.

Olson, Roger E. *The Mosaic of Christian Belief: Twenty Centuries of Unity and Diversity.* 2nd ed. Downers Grove, IL: IVP Academic, 2016.

Placher, William C. *A History of Christian Theology: An Introduction.* 2nd ed. Philadelphia: Westminster, 2013.

Torrance, Thomas F. *The Trinitarian Faith: The Evangelical Theology of the Ancient Catholic Church.* 2nd ed. New York: Bloomsbury T&T Clark, 2016.

Woodbridge, John D., and Frank A. James III. *From Pre-Reformation to the Present Day: The Rise and Growth of the Church in Its Cultural, Intellectual, and Political Context.* Vol. 2 of *Church History.* Grand Rapids: Zondervan, 2013.

How to Dialogue with a Theological Work

Written "Dialogues" should be thorough, yet concise, and answer the following questions:

Context
- When was the work originally written? Who originally published the work?
- What is the specific context of the work?
  - What is the specific social, political, and religious context?
- Why did the author(s) write this work?
  - What is the specific reason, and who is the specific audience?
- What is the author's background?
  - What is the author's specific religious affiliation/ denomination, education, ethnicity, and so forth?

Framework and Sources
- What type of theological work is it? Identify whether it is a sermon, theological treatise, polemic, response, commentary, systematic work, satire, story/novel, poem, autobiography, and so forth.

- What theological method does the author utilize? Identify the specific method (dialectic, experimental/rational, feminist, historical-critical, literal exegetical, narrative, postmodern, revisionist, reader-response, other).
- What are the author's presuppositions? An author's presuppositions include their views about where we came from, who God is, who we are, what is wrong, what is the remedy, what is authoritative, etc.
- What sources does the author credit or infer for intellectual ideas and critical assistance? Reason, science, philosophy, Scripture, experience? What specific parts of Scripture?

Thesis and Key Points

- What is the work's main thesis? Try to restate the thesis in your own words in ten to twelve words or less.
- What are the five to seven key points/arguments of the work?

Define Key Terms (according to the author's usage)

- Define words that are unfamiliar.
- Define words important to the argument, even if you think you know what they mean. For example, define Martin Luther's specific understanding of *sola scriptura*.

Assessment

- Note insights, questions, and critiques of the work.
- What is your view of the work? Give specific areas of agreement or disagreement, and note why you agree or disagree.
- How well do the author's specific views accord with Scripture? Be specific here, giving examples.
- Identify what the text teaches about God, ourselves, and the world.
- Give specific implications of this work for Christianity, for society, and for yourself.

A Guide for Participating in a Theological Discussion

A theological discussion can help us think analytically, express ideas effectively, and listen attentively to a theological text in a community setting. Theological works are important because they force us to think about significant questions: Who is God? Who are we? What can we know? How should we act? What can we hope for? The better we understand the answers, the better equipped we are to know God, ourselves, and the world around us and how we should live our lives in submission to Christ.

The role of the leader is to ask questions that help the group explore the ideas in the work. The leader is not permitted to give answers. The participants may also ask questions and offer answers. All answers must be based on the reading of the text; no references are to be made to outside sources (except other works previously discussed and the Bible). The leader will encourage participants to agree or disagree with what the author and other participants say and ask them to back up opinions with reasons based on the text and Scripture.

DISCUSSION PRINCIPLES

Read in advance. In order to participate, you must complete the reading and outline it. Read carefully. Although the discussions

173

are not intended to be merely an exercise in memory, you will not get much out of them unless you accurately remember what you have read. Read the entire work, or at least portions of it, more than once. Mark passages and make comments in the margins. Some of the things you should underline and write down are:

- ideas in the work you consider essential
- words or passages you do not understand
- passages with which you agree or disagree
- passages about which you would like to hear the opinions of others
- passages on which you would like to comment in light of Scripture or your own experience
- passages that relate to other Christian works your group has read and discussed

Take time to reflect. Pick out a few of the ideas, concepts, or examples that interest you most. Try to increase your understanding of them by restating the ideas in your own words or by imagining how you would respond to the same questions addressed in the text. Finally, write down any new ideas about the work that occur to you as a result of this exercise.

Discuss only the reading. Every moment of the discussion is needed to cover the ideas in the work. Avoid introducing ideas or personal experiences that have nothing to do with the text. By discussing only the work that everyone has read, each person will be able to follow and take part in the discussion. Leave the names of critics and experts out of the discussion.

Back up your statements. Avoid judging a statement by who makes it or who agrees with it, but rather judge it by how well it is supported. Statements are well-supported in the discussion by:

- directly referencing the work
- giving an accurate summary of what the work says
- offering reasons or examples from Scripture

Stick to the subject under discussion. You should work together to fully explore each question. Try to find new ideas about what is being discussed. Avoid continuing to talk after you have made your point or making a comment that no longer fits into the discussion. You will not receive credit for adding to the discussion if you do not add illumination to the issue.

Strive for understanding. Explore the meanings of the work as fully as possible, trying to resolve the issues that are raised, but realizing that not all issues can be resolved to everyone's satisfaction.

Speak up freely. Say what you think, and be ready to give your reasons. You may agree or disagree with anything said by your fellow participants. Be sure to make your statements or ask your questions to them rather than to the leader. You do not need to wait to be called on.

Listen carefully. When others speak, do not pay so much attention to your own thoughts that you fail to hear what is said. Question them about any remark you don't understand before you contribute your ideas.

Be courteous. Speak clearly so that your remarks may be heard by everyone in the room. Do not interrupt someone when she is speaking. Avoid criticizing a person; instead critique the ideas they present. Do not engage in private conversations. Give the leader and your fellow participants the same respect and attention you would like for yourself.

Point of order. Anyone can call a point of order, but must not interrupt a sentence.

- "I can't follow; there's too much chaos."
- "Help, I don't understand what was just said [or something from the work]" or "I'm lost in the discussion."

- "How does what we're on help answer the question?"
- "We've answered that question."
- "You repeated what I said."

How to Lead a Theological Discussion

Reflective thinking exercise. The leader is to facilitate an exercise in reflective thinking that will help increase the group's understanding of the work by doing the following things:

- developing your own questions rather than going to online or other sources
- asking questions that initiate, sustain, and conclude investigations into ideas and problems in the text
- asking questions that explore unclear, factually incorrect, or contradictory statements
- evaluating responses and selecting statements to question immediately—ignoring those that are trivial and tabling some for later

Read carefully. A careful reading of the text will allow you to develop questions from the following sources:

- ideas in the work you consider interesting or important
- words or passages you do not understand
- passages that have multiple meanings and implications
- interconnecting ideas in the work

- passages whose truthfulness or application should be considered in the light of Scripture

Types of questions. There are three main types of questions you can ask about the work:

- *Questions of fact.* Factual questions have one correct answer. These include questions regarding definitions, the background of the work/author, and details of the text. They require the participant to offer quotations from or paraphrases of the work in response to them.
    - *Example:* What analogies does Cyprian use in *On the Unity of the Church* to demonstrate the church's unity while being dispersed throughout the world?
- *Questions of interpretation.* Interpretative questions explore what the author means by what he or she says. They are open-ended, can lead to an extended discussion of ideas in the text, and can elicit multiple responses.
    - *Example:* What is the primary reason Cyprian is arguing that church unity is essential? In other words, is it an issue of correct theology, right polity, a defense against heresy, related to salvation, or another reason?
- *Questions of assessment.* Assessment questions, which include evaluative and application questions, require the reader to assess the veracity and value of the work and the extent to which the work has application to his or her own life, the church, and the world.
    - *Example:* How well does Cyprian's stance on church unity accord with Psalm 133; John 17:20–23; 1 Corinthians 1:10–17; and Ephesians 4:1–16? What should church unity be based on?

Formatting questions. Seek to formulate open-ended questions, avoiding yes and no questions. Also table opinion questions until you have explored what the work says and what the work means.

The basic question. The BQ is always an open-ended interpretive question that can lead to an extended discussion of what you consider to be one of the main ideas of the work. A robust BQ should generate opposing or different responses, which will help to clarify and develop the ideas you believe are important to the work. You should begin the discussion with the BQ and go back to it when you need to refocus the conversation.

The follow-ups. The follow-ups help unpack the BQ. They are comprised of factual and interpretive questions that explore possible responses to the BQ, key terms, ideas, sources the author uses, the context, and the author's background.

The evaluative questions. Evaluative questions explore how the participant agrees or disagrees with the author's ideas or the extent to which the work has application to his or her own life.

Favor questions of interpretation. Interpretive questions help increase a deeper understanding of the work. If the group is not accurately remembering what the author said or is offering incorrect interpretations, however, ask questions of fact. Questions of evaluation are meaningful only after the group has thoroughly discussed related questions of interpretation. While evaluative questions may get a discussion started, they can quickly turn it into a polling of likes and dislikes, or a defense of premature or hasty judgments. To avoid this, questions of evaluation should always deal with the truth or the application of ideas from the work. They should not be allowed to lead to a discussion of subjects that do not require the use of the work; otherwise, the discussion loses its purpose and becomes a recital of opinions about abstract terms, topical events, or unsubstantiated ideas.

Discuss the work ahead of time with your coleader or a friend. Alternating as participant and leader, try to answer your set of questions. Sharpen the questions you believe will promote a profitable examination of the work. Delete questions that do not seem to go anywhere. Write down new questions that arise from your discussion.

Know when to ask follow-up questions. Follow-up questions contain ideas that are subordinate but related to the BQ. Their primary function is to help the group resolve the BQ. Follow-up questions are used to:

- introduce some of the implications of the BQ
- require a participant to substantiate a statement or opinion
- elicit more responses about the subject being discussed
- clarify a statement
- develop the most important ideas in a participant's response
- encourage participants to examine the consequences and consistency of their remarks
- bring the discussion back to the work

Ask assessment questions at the end of the discussion. Avoid asking assessment questions prior to asking the BQ and the follow-ups.

Strive for answers. Avoid being content with superficial responses or attempts by the participants to leave a question just because it is difficult. Use their answers as the basis for new questions that will help the group reach a deeper understanding of the work. Yet keep in mind that some questions asked will not be answered to everyone's satisfaction.

Avoid difficult or technical questions. Questions such as, What is supralapsarianism? when the term is not in the work interrupt the group's exploration of the author's meaning by diverting their attention to words that cannot be defined in context.

Word your questions carefully. Ask one question at a time, and keep your questions brief and clear. Try to ask questions tailored to the work, avoiding questions that indicate the answers you expect or that are yes and no questions, cannot be answered, or force the participant to draw on outside material not assigned.

Listen intently. This will help you ask relevant follow-up questions. It will also give you ideas for other questions and indicate whether particular lines of inquiry should be abandoned.

Involve each participant. Invite participants into the discussion by prefacing your questions with their name. Make sure questions are directed to *every* participant during each meeting. Encourage participants to ask each other questions and to speak freely without raising their hands or waiting to be acknowledged by the leaders.

Observe the basic principles of discussion. These rules help the participants think for themselves and ensure maximum use of the time for discussion of the works.

- Principle 1: No participant who has not read and outlined the work may take part in the discussion.
- Principle 2: The group may discuss only the work assigned or works read/discussed for previous sessions.
- Principle 3: Participants may not introduce outside authorities, except the Bible or previous readings, to lend weight to their opinions.
- Principle 4: As a leader, you may only ask questions. Avoid inserting your opinions or comments.
- Principle 5: All participants need to show respect to each other and the leaders.

Theological Discussion Questions on Cyprian's *On the Unity of the Church*

Develop discussion questions following the format below. Avoid yes and no questions and opinion questions for the BQ and the follow-up questions. Include page numbers whenever possible to help refer the group back to the text.

BASIC QUESTION

What is the primary reason Cyprian is arguing that church unity is essential? In other words, is it an issue of correct theology, right polity, a defense against heresy, related to salvation, or another reason?

FOLLOW-UPS

1. How did the context of persecution and the Novatian schism set the stage for this work?
2. What is unity based on, according to Cyprian?

3. What kind of a hierarchical structure is Cyprian promoting? Monepiscopacy or episcopacy? How does he view Peter? What is the role of the bishop?

4. How does Cyprian argue from Scripture that the true church is united in one body of bishops?

5. How does this idea impact his understanding of what to do in response to apostates?

6. What analogies does Cyprian use to demonstrate the church's unity while being dispersed throughout the world?

7. What does Cyprian mean by "Do not think that good people can depart from the Church"? What is the relationship between being "good" and being part of the church?

8. Cyprian writes, "No one can have God for his Father, who does not have the Church for his mother." What does he mean by this?

9. What is the main determining factor of the "true church" for Cyprian?

ASSESSMENT

1. How well does Cyprian's stance on church unity accord with Psalm 133; John 17:20–23; 1 Corinthians 1:10–17; Ephesians 4:1–16? What should church unity be based on?

2. What constitutes the true church, according to Scripture?

3. How should we view a person who has read God's Word, put their faith in Christ apart from other believers, and then led others to faith and started worshiping together without church leadership?

4. What is the purpose and role of the church in a believer's life? In conveying grace?

5. What is your perspective on church governance and discipline? What role has it played in your life?

Glossary

Disclaimer: Theological words can have a number of different meanings that are often dependent on who is using them. This glossary is an attempt to give general definitions for some common theological terms that are used this text. One must remember, however, when trying to understand a theological word, it's always best to go back to the source to determine the author's meaning, rather than consulting a standard dictionary or glossary. The words below are taken from the chapters, and the definitions are those used by the author of this book.

Anthropocentric. A human-centered perspective of the world.

Anthropology. The doctrine of humanity is often seen as a subtopic of the doctrine of creation. It includes the origin of humanity, the image of God in humanity, gender, the constitutional nature of humans, and the purpose of life.

Apocrypha. In Greek, *apocrypha* means "hidden or secret things." More commonly, it refers to fifteen additional books included in the Roman Catholic Bible.

Apologetic. Theological works written in defense of the Christian faith.

Apologist. Defends the Christian faith through systematic, argumentative, or pragmatic discourse.

Arianism. The nontrinitarian Christological heresy that originated with the Alexandrian priest Arius in the third century that denies the divinity and eternality of Christ. Arianism maintains that Jesus Christ was created and is subordinate to the Father.

Arminianism. A theological view named after Jacobus Arminius (1560–1609) that affirms that humanity retains libertarian free will after the fall based on God's grace. In contrast to Calvinism, it maintains universal prevenient grace, conditional election based on foreseen faith, unlimited (universal) atonement, resistible grace, and uncertainty of perseverance.

Biblical literalism (biblicism). Approaches reading the Bible by prioritizing the literal interpretation over allegorical interpretation, seeing Scripture as generally speaking about real historic events and needed to be understood as literal statements by the author. Generally, it takes into account figures of speech and various literary forms.

Biblical theologian. Seeks to discover what the biblical writers, such as John or Paul, under divine guidance, believed, described, and taught in the context of their own historical setting. It is primarily a descriptive type of theology.

Biblical veracity. Referring to the truthfulness of Scripture.

Calvinism. A theological view named after John Calvin (1509–1564) that emphasizes human depravity and God's sovereign rule over everything. The five points of Calvinism, in contrast to Arminianism, are total depravity, unconditional election, limited atonement, irresistible grace, and perseverance of the saints.

Catechism. Summary of the principles of faith in the form of questions and answers that is used for the instruction of Christians.

Catholic. The term *catholic* with a lower c refers to universal. "Catholic" refers to the Roman Catholic Church.

Cessationism. The view that miraculous gifts of the Holy Spirit, such as prophecy and speaking in tongues, are limited to the time of the apostles when they were establishing the church, prior to the completion of the canon of Scripture.

Christian humanism. A perspective popularized during the Renaissance that emphasized human dignity, potential, and the individual conscience and placed emphasis on going back to original sources, especially Scripture, and studying it in the original languages.

Christology. The doctrine of Christ includes the person (nature) and work of Jesus Christ.

Classical Inerrantist (biblical inerrantist). The understanding of inspiration and inerrancy as expressed in the 1949 Evangelical Theological Society doctrinal statement and the Chicago Statement on Biblical Inerrancy in 1978 that affirms the "total inerrancy of Scripture" and the inspiration process as extending to the very words of Scripture. The Bible is a universal, indisputable basis for human knowledge.

Commentary. A systematic series of explanations of the background and meaning of biblical passages. Typically they are organized by book, chapter, and verse.

Common grace. A term used by Reformed thinkers to describe God's grace that is common or available to all humankind and is not related to salvation.

Continuationism. The view that the miraculous gifts spoken about in the book of Acts, such as healing, speaking in tongues, and prophecy, are normative gifts given by the Holy Spirit and available today.

Correlational approach. The pursuit of truth by discovering the correlation between Christian revelation and issues raised by the contemporary understanding of human existence. Revelation must speak to and make sense of the current situation. Revisionist theology would fall under this category.

Council of Nicaea. Also known as the First Council of Nicaea (AD 325). This was the first recognized ecumenical council of the Christian church called by Roman emperor Constantine I. It condemned the teachings of Arius that deemed Christ as inferior to God and established the doctrine of the Trinity.

Creed/Confession of faith. Formal declaration of principal articles of faith or mission of a church or religious group.

Denomination. A recognized branch of the Christian church that adheres to set beliefs or a common identity.

Depravity. The inherent sinful nature or bent to sin in all people, inherited from Adam and his fall.

Devotional work. Christian literature that is written for spiritual formation and growth.

Diabolical. A term indicating something is evil or bad and not leading to true knowledge and worship of God.

Dialectic. A theological analysis including a dialogue with or reaction to a specific idea or theological work. It may be written in a question/answer or dialogue format. Medieval Scholastics and neoorthodox theologians often used this genre.

Discernment. The ability to distinguish between truth and error. Christian discernment is being able to think biblically about everything.

Divine foreknowledge. God's infallible knowledge before the creation of the world of salvation of individuals.

Divine inspiration. A term indicating that the words of Scripture are "God-breathed" or are spoken by God.

Doctrine. A biblical belief or teaching. It comes from the Greek word meaning "that which is taught" and generally refers to the set of teachings to be held by Christians.

Doctrine of the Christian life. The doctrine of the Christian life includes the topics of discipleship, obedience, holiness, sanctification, perseverance, and Christian virtues and ethics.

Doctrine of creation. Includes the creation of the world and the cosmos, God's relation to creation, the state of the original creation, the Sabbath, the impact of the fall on creation, angels, and creation care.

Dogma. A synonym for the term *doctrine.*

Ecclesiology. The doctrine of the church, which includes the nature of the church, the purpose of the church, the power of the church, the role and government of the church, the ordinances (sacraments) of the church (including baptism and the Lord's Supper), and worship in the church.

Elect. Those chosen by God for salvation before the creation of the world.

Eschatology. The doctrine of the future includes death, the second coming of Christ, views on the millennium and tribulation, the final judgment and eternal punishment, and the new heaven and new earth.

Eucharist. Another word for the Lord's Supper.

Evangelical. The term generally refers to the teaching of the gospel. Specifically, it refers to a member of the Evangelical tradition.

Evolutionary creationist. The view that the triune God created the universe and all of life through a God-ordained, sustained, and design-reflecting evolutionary process.

Exegesis. The process of biblical interpretation by thoroughly analyzing a text.

Experiential/Experimental approach. The pursuit of truth by immediate interaction of the soul with God or by natural religious consciousness. Religious feelings, intuition, or rational experiences of the individual are seen as the normative source of truth, rather than the Bible alone. This approach assumes that truth can be discovered in the realm of human experience. Protestant liberalism and mysticism could be placed under this approach.

Feminist theology. A movement that seeks to reconsider Scripture, Christianity, and its practices from a feminist perspective.

Free will. When used in respect to mankind, it refers to the ability to make and enact noncontingent choices.

Hamartiology. The doctrine of the fall and sin is often seen as a subtopic of anthropology. It includes the doctrine of evil and an understanding of the fall, the consequences of the fall, the nature of sin, the source of sin, humanity's relationship with Adam, the results of sin, and the individual and social dimensions of sin.

Heresy. An unbiblical belief contrary to an essential orthodox doctrine of the Christian faith.

Historical approach. The pursuit of truth by understanding the world behind the text. It assumes historical analysis is necessary for understanding the past and uncovering the true message of Scripture. Some liberal theologians could be placed under this approach.

Historical-critical approach. The interpretation of Scripture through the historical investigation of what actually happened or was alluded to in the passage. This approach often examines Scripture in a "purely scientific" manner, excluding a supernatural perspective.

Historical theologian. Investigates the development of Christian thought through the centuries since Bible times.

Ideological theologian. Explores the relationship between Christian theology and particular ideologies. It puts a particular emphasis on doing theology from a specific perspective, often of the oppressed, and recognizes the need for upholding social justice and human rights and seeing Jesus as Savior and Liberator. This would include liberation, black, and feminist theologies.

Incarnation. The act of God by which the Son of God, Jesus Christ (the Word), became flesh (human).

Inerrancy. Scripture is free from falsehood or mistake, being without error in the original manuscripts.

Infallibility. The message of Scripture is neither misleading nor misled and is the rule and guide in all matters, giving a reliable testimony to salvation and is the norm for faith and life.

Justification. God's work of making the sinner right with God through Christ's atoning work, thereby removing the guilt and penalty of sin and declaring one right in God's sight.

Liberation theology. It puts a particular emphasis on doing theology from the specific perspective of the oppressed and recognizes the need for upholding social justice and human rights and seeing Jesus as Savior and Liberator. This would include liberation, black, and feminist theologians.

Literal exegetical approach. Seeks to interpret Scripture according to the simple, plain meaning of the text.

Monism. The view that mankind is comprised of only one part —the physical body.

Moral theologian (practical ethicist). Examines the relationship between the Bible and real-life situations, problems, and needs, including topics such as medical and sexual ethics.

Mystical. Describes an experiential knowledge of God, often including ecstatic visions of God and descriptions of the soul's union with God.

Mysticism. The practice of experiential knowledge and love of God, with the ultimate aim of union with God.

Neoorthodox approach. The pursuit of truth by encountering God in the Word. In contrast to propositionalism (that prioritizes the Bible) and experientialism (that prioritizes reason/experience), it emphasizes the revelation of God himself as the foundation of Christian beliefs. The Bible is regarded as an instrument that is a witness to the true Word of God—Jesus Christ. This approach often seeks to find truth in opposites and paradoxes.

Nonreductive physicalism. A philosophical view that identifies mental properties as being not identical to physical properties, yet not separable from the physical body.

Open theism. This view, also known as openness theology, holds that God does not know the future in exhaustive detail but leaves it partially "open" (not settled) to "possibilities" or "maybes" that are determined by a creature's free acts.

Original sin. The first sin of the first man, Adam, which resulted in human depravity and guilt for the human race.

Orthodox. The term *orthodox* comes from the Greek and means "correct thinking." When used with a lowercase *o*, it refers to views adhering to the traditional historic Christian faith. Orthodox with an uppercase *O* refers to the Eastern Orthodox or the Oriental Orthodox churches.

Philosophical theologian. Utilizes philosophical reflection, language, and methods in the process of doing theology, with the aim of having a theoretical understanding of the nature and character of God and God's relationship with the world.

Pluralism. The recognition of the value of the diversity of religious beliefs, practices, and traditions. Within pluralism are a variety of different perspectives on their value—from a recognition that some truth exists in various religious traditions to the belief that no one tradition is superior to another.

Pneumatology. The doctrine of the Holy Spirit, which includes the person and work of the Holy Spirit.

Polemic. A theological argument addressing an important, controversial topic often written as an attack or a defense of a belief.

Postconservative approach. The pursuit of truth by moving beyond a propositional theology, while still centering theology on the Bible. It often defers to tradition and orthodox doctrine critically and constructively.

Postliberalism (narrative approach). The pursuit of truth by utilizing a cultural-linguistic approach to theology. Doctrines are seen as shaping and providing the structure for individual religious experience. It emphasizes the authority of the person of Christ and the biblical narratives over the historic truthfulness or inerrancy of Scripture. The focus is primarily on the beliefs and practices of the Christian community.

Postmodernism. A system of thought that denies objective truth and absolutes.

Practical theologian. The practical theologian focuses on the pastoral application of biblical truths in modern life.

Pragmatism. An approach that determines the truth based on the practical consequences.

Praxis approach. The pursuit of truth by seeing the current reality as foundational. Interpretation begins and ends with the current social reality. This approach is often committed to the struggle for justice and practical concerns shape the reading and interpreting of Scripture. Liberation, feminist, black, *mujerista*, and womanist theologies could fall under this orientation.

Presupposition. A control belief or an implicit assumption.

Prolegomena. All introductory matters of theology, including the nature and task of theology and issues regarding how to do theology (methodology), how to acquire knowledge (epistemology), and what the sources of theology are.

Propositional approach (rationalist propositional). The pursuit of truth by uncovering the theologian's intended meaning of the text. It sees the task as to gather biblical data and formulate theological principles from the information. Scripture is generally seen as the foundation for theology. It is often assumed it can be accessed and interpreted by reason. Conservative Evangelicalism and Fundamentalism are often associated with this approach.

Protestantism. A Christian movement that emerged out of a break with the Roman Catholic Church in Europe in the early sixteenth century over disagreements concerning matters of faith and practice.

Reader-response approach. An interpretive approach that views the reader as the active agent who imparts "real existence" to biblical text and gives it meaning through interpreting it.

Reformed. Reformed teachings are rooted in the sixteenth-century Protestant Reformation and emphasize the sovereignty of God, the authority of Scripture, the need for pursuing holiness, and the lordship of Christ over all creation.

Revelation. The doctrine includes how God reveals God's nature, will, and truth. It includes the nature and purpose of general and special revelation, the preservation of revelation, and the dependability of God's Word.

Revisionist theology. Sees the main task of theology as exploring the critical correlation between human experiences and the texts of the Christian tradition.

Sacred. The quality of being holy or set apart.

Sermon. An oration expounding on biblical passages or theological topics.

Sitz im Leben. A German phrase ("setting in life") used in biblical criticism that refers to the social setting of a text.

Sola scriptura. A Latin phrase that means Scripture alone is sufficient for faith and practice and the supreme authority in spiritual matters.

Soteriology. The doctrine of salvation, which includes God's plan for salvation, God's provision of salvation in history, God's application of salvation to the individual, and God's completion of salvation.

Systematic. A systematic study of what the Bible teaches on various topics in Scripture.

Systematic approach. The pursuit of truth through faith and human reason. It aims at developing a logically coherent and rationally defensible system, derived from deductions based on known precepts. Medieval Scholasticism and Protestant Scholasticism can be placed under this approach.

Systematic theologian. Attempts to express in unified constructs the biblical teaching on theological topics such as the doctrine of Christ, anthropology, or the Trinity.

Theological treatise. An in-depth exposition or argument treating a theological topic in depth and investigating the principles of the topic.

Theology proper. The study of God, which includes the existence and knowledge of God, the nature of God, the work of God, and the Trinity.

Total depravity. The Reformed doctrine that holds that as a consequence of the fall, human nature is thoroughly corrupt and guilty and unable apart from grace to be saved.

Tradition. A doctrinal belief held to have authority through the handing down from the apostles, though it is not contained in Scripture.

Trinity. The doctrine affirmed in the Nicene Creed that holds that God eternally exists as three co-equal, co-eternal divine persons—Father, Son, and Holy Spirit.

Vulgate. Jerome's Latin version of the Bible.

Well-versed inerrancy. A view that holds that biblical authors speak truth in everything they affirm.

Wesleyan quadrilateral. A term coined by Albert Outler that refers to a methodology utilizing four different sources—Scripture, tradition, reason, and experience—to come to theological conclusions.

General Index

Adam. *See* historical Adam
Adler, Mortimer, 10, 12, 86, 111,
   112, 114, 122, 128, 143
Anderson, Ray S., 77
Anselm, 79, 97, 139–40, 160
anthropocentric, 141–42, 185
anthropology, 42, 74, 77, 142,
   185
Apocrypha, 93, 119, 185
apologetics, 15, 16, 69, 76, 78,
   80, 185
apologist. *See* apologetics.
Apostles' Creed, 79
Aquinas, Thomas, 77
Arianism, 186
Aristotle, 98
Arius, 186, 188
Arminianism, 85, 186
Athanasius, 38
Augustine, xiv, 34–35, 45, 77,
   80, 103, 106
autobiography, 80, 171

baptism, 74, 94–95, 190
Barth, Karl, 77, 79, 84, 92
Baxter, Richard, 77
Berkhof, Louis, 77

biblical literalism, 64–65, 81,
   93, 118n16, 172, 186, 192
biblical theologian, 77, 186
biblical veracity, 132, 186
biography, 7, 80
Bird, Michael, 120–21
body of Christ, 6, 10, 24
Boyd, Gregory A., 44–45, 47–48,
   75
Brueggemann, Walter, 157–58
Bunyan, John, 79

Calvin, John, 3, 39, 57, 77, 79, 97,
   103, 137, 186
Calvinism, 11, 45, 61, 186
Carson, D. A., 77
catechism, 16, 79, 94, 187
Catholicism, 5, 35, 36, 61, 62,
   91, 94–95, 99, 100, 119,
   185, 187, 195
cessationism, 55, 187
Challies, Tim, 2–3, 27
Christ. *See* Jesus.
Christian humanism, 62, 112, 187
Christian life, 16, 41, 74, 142, 189
Christology, 73, 142, 187
classical inerrantism, 93, 121, 187

commentary, 16, 79, 171, 187
common grace, 135, 188
Cone, James, 78
confession of faith, 16, 57, 79,
    94, 95, 113, 141, 188
continuationism, 55, 188
correlational approach, 16, 84,
    188, 196
Council of Nicaea, 38, 188
Craig, William Lane, 45, 78
Creator, 3, 135, 150
creed, 16, 79, 94, 95, 141, 188

Damasio, Antonio, 90
Darwinism, 105
denominations, 15, 40, 60, 69,
    171, 188
depravity, 24, 85, 119, 134, 186,
    188, 193, 197
Descartes, René, 90–91, 144
devotional, 16, 77, 80, 188
diabolical, 2, 189
dialectic, 79, 157, 172, 189
discernment, xiv, 4, 5–7, 10, 11,
    18, 20, 22, 23, 26, 29, 96,
    127, 128, 157–58, 189
divine foreknowledge, 43–45,
    47–48, 74–75, 115, 189
divine inspiration, 54, 93, 187, 189
doctrine, 2, 16, 18, 57, 58,
    73–75, 84, 97n15, 121,
    127–28, 143, 189
doctrine of creation, xiii, 16,
    64–65, 73–75, 84, 101,
    115, 134–135, 139, 189
dogma, 141–43, 189
dualism, 104–5

Eastern Orthodoxy, 36, 59, 61,
    94, 193

ecclesiology, 74, 190
Eddy, Mary Baker, 133–35
Edwards, Jonathan, 6, 77, 78,
    85, 98
Ehrman, Bart, 92
elect, 43, 186, 190
election. See elect.
Eliot, George, 32, 93n9
Elwell, Walter A., 65
Enns, Peter, 120–21
Erasmus, 79, 80, 87, 112, 113,
    119–20, 122
Erickson, Millard, 77
eschatology, 74, 142, 190
ethics, 74, 77, 142, 189, 192
Eucharist, 119, 190
Evangelical, 36, 42, 43–45, 56,
    61, 63–65, 82, 99, 117–22,
    187, 190, 195
Evans, Rachel Held, 118
evil, 74, 189, 191
evolutionary creationism,
    64–65, 190
evolutionism, 63–65, 100, 105,
    190
exegetical approach, 172, 192
experience, 16, 46, 60–61, 67, 79,
    80, 82–83, 84, 91, 98–99,
    132, 138, 172, 190, 193,
    194, 196, 198
experiential approach, 16, 72,
    80, 82, 83, 85, 134, 190
experimental approach, 82, 172,
    190

fall, the, 16, 26, 73–74, 97–98,
    103, 106, 114, 115, 135,
    139, 142, 186, 188, 189,
    191, 197
fallibility, 54

feminist theologians, 61, 78, 81n2, 83, 172, 191, 192, 195
Fiorenza, Elisabeth Schüssler, 35
frame of reference, 15, 53, 59–61
Franke, John, 121
freedom, 53, 61, 75
free will, xiv, 105, 115, 137, 186, 191
Frost, Robert, 52–53, 66, 68
Fundamentalism, 82, 100, 117, 195

gender, 42, 46, 61, 74, 77, 87, 101, 185
gifts of the Holy Spirit, 56, 187
Gladwell, Malcom, 19
God
  grace of, 55, 85, 95, 115, 120, 135, 186, 188, 197
  image of in humanity, 74, 96, 134, 185
  knowledge of, xv, 3–4, 7, 23–24, 73, 80, 84, 136, 137, 142, 193
  mercy of, 24, 26, 115, 134
  nature of, 2, 73, 197
  sovereignty of, 75, 85, 140, 186, 196
  will of, 26, 85, 139–40, 144
  work of, 73, 197
Grenz, Stanley, 84
Gunkel, Hermann, 54
Gutiérrez, Gustavo, 78, 101–2

hamartiology, 74, 191
Hamilton, Alexander, 98
Hauerwas, Stanley, 77
Heidelberg Catechism, 79
heresy, 27, 38, 66, 155, 178, 183, 186, 191

historical Adam, 64–65, 74, 114, 115, 188, 191, 193
historical approach, 83, 191
historical-critical approach, 141, 172, 191
historical theologian, 77, 191
Hitchcock, Christina, 41–42
Holy Spirit, xv, 4, 6, 13, 16, 18–19, 25, 27–28, 55–56, 73, 94–95, 128, 132, 138, 187, 188, 194, 197
House, H. Wayne, 65

ideological theologian, 15, 78, 81, 191
incarnation, 192
inerrancy, 44, 84, 93, 119, 120–22, 187, 192, 194, 198
infallibility, 93, 121, 189, 192

Jesus, 4, 11, 16, 24, 28, 38, 47, 62, 73, 78, 84, 130–31, 140–41, 142–43, 148, 186, 187, 192, 193, 197
Johnson, Elizabeth A., 46, 83
Julian of Norwich, 80, 98–99
justification, 5, 192
Justin Martyr, 78, 80

Kapic, Kelly, 138
Kavanaugh, J. F., 135
Ken, Thomas, 80
King Jr., Martin Luther, 78
kingdom of God, 142–43
knowledge of self, 3, 7, 23–24, 136, 137

Lamoureux, Denis, 62–65, 66
Langer, Richard, 12n5

Lewis, C. S., 25, 38, 40, 78; 98, 149–50
liberation theologian, 61, 102n17, 192
Lindbeck, George, 84
literal exegetical method, 172, 192
Lord's Supper, 62, 74, 94, 190
Luther, Martin, 5, 11, 37, 39, 46, 60, 62, 78, 91, 97, 113, 119–20, 172
Lutheranism, 36, 61, 95, 143

Machen, J. Gresham, 92
Mathison, Keith, 59, 96n12
McGrath, Alister, 77
memoir, 16, 34, 80
Merida, Tony, 7
Milton, John, 80, 114, 115
Mohler, Albert, 121
monism, 104, 192
moral theologian, 77, 192
Moreland, J. P., 41
Murphy, Nancey, 100, 104–6
mysticism, 16, 80, 83, 85, 99, 131, 190, 193

narrative approach, 14, 27, 47–48, 54, 84, 85, 93, 172, 194
neoorthodox approach, 16, 83, 189, 193
Nietzsche, Friedrich, 137
nonreductive physicalism, 105, 193
Nouwen, Henri, 22

O'Connor, Flannery, 150
O'Donovan, Oliver, 77
open theism, 44–45, 47–48, 193
original sin, 119, 193
Orthodox Church, 58–59

orthodoxy, 18, 38, 44–45, 84, 139, 191, 193, 194
Osteen, Joel, 101–2
Outler, Albert C., 91, 198

Packer, J. I., 79, 140
Pelikan, Jaroslav, 77
perseverance, 74, 186, 189
philosophical theologian, 14, 15, 40, 59, 77, 85, 194
Piper, John, 75
Plantinga, Alvin, 77
pluralism, 56, 194
pneumatology, 73, 194
polemic, 16, 72, 78, 171, 194
postconservative approach, 16, 84
postliberalism, 16, 84
postmodernism, 172, 194
practical theologian, 59, 77, 195
pragmatism, 61, 78, 186, 195
praxis approach, 16, 83, 102n17, 195
prayer, 22–27, 29, 94, 128–29, 144, 151
presuppositions, 15, 54, 58, 59–60, 61–65, 72, 98, 105, 119, 129, 132, 172, 195
prolegomena, 73, 195
propositional approach, 16, 82, 85, 93, 113, 115, 150, 195
Protestantism, 29, 39, 58–59, 83, 87, 96, 107, 117, 190, 195, 196, 197

race, 46, 61, 77
rationalism, 82, 91, 98, 149–50, 195
reader-response, 172, 196
reason, 16, 56, 62, 82, 83, 90–91, 96–98, 105,

142–43, 149, 155, 172, 193, 195, 197, 198
redemption, xv, 74, 115, 139
Reformed theology, 35, 36, 58–59, 188, 196, 197
revelation, 16, 19, 23–25, 62, 73, 83–84, 92, 96, 103, 106, 135, 142, 188, 193, 196
revisionism, 61, 84, 172, 188, 196
Roman Catholic. *See* Catholicism.

salvation, 16, 23–24, 28, 55, 74, 117, 135, 142–43, 155, 178, 189, 190, 192, 196
sanctification, 25, 29, 74, 150, 189
Sanders, Fred, 35–36
satire, 16, 79, 80, 87, 171
Sayers, Dorothy, 10n1, 80
Schleiermacher, Friedrich, 83, 91, 99
Scofield Study Bible, 79
sermons, 10, 16, 72, 78, 85, 171, 196
sin, 16, 28, 74, 98, 119, 131, 132, 188, 191, 192, 193
Sitz im Leben, 53–54
Socrates, 149
sola scriptura, 58–59, 66, 91, 92–93, 103, 172, 196
Sölle, Dorothee, 78
soteriology, 74, 142, 196
spiritual formation, 80, 188
Spurgeon, Charles, 77, 148
systematic approach, 16, 78, 79, 83, 186, 187, 197
systematic theologian, 15, 77, 197

systematic works, 39–40, 72, 79, 171, 197

Tannen, Deborah, 12–13
theological treatise, 16, 78, 85, 171, 197
theology proper, 73, 197
Thielicke, Helmut, 2, 11, 149
Tillich, Paul, 77, 84
total depravity. *See* depravity.
Tozer, A. W., 80
tradition, xiv, 16, 62, 84, 91, 94–96, 106, 107, 190, 194, 196, 197, 198
Trinity, 35–36, 38, 63, 73, 77, 119, 142, 188, 197
Turretin, Francis, 35, 83

Vanhoozer, Kevin, 121, 128
virtues, 74, 189
Von Harnack, Adolf, 47, 75, 83, 141–43
Vos, Geerhardus, 77
Vulgate, 29, 119, 197
Vygotsky, Lev, 151

well-versed inerrancy, 121, 198
Wesleyan quadrilateral, 91, 198
Whitehead, Alfred North, 66–67
wisdom, xiv, 2–4, 10, 13–14, 24, 26, 91n3, 111, 132, 137, 148–50, 156
worldliness, 132
worship, 24, 26, 74, 80, 94–95, 136–37, 138, 144, 189, 190
Wright, N. T., 77

Zwingli, Ulrich, 62, 92, 97